MW01230503

PARADISE EARNED
A Fifty-Year Voyage

SCOTT HIRSCH

A Fifty Year Voyage

May 22nd, 1976, Summer Before Junior Year of High School.
(Or very close to that date)

"We got no choice
All the girls and boys
School's out for summer."
−Alice Cooper, 1972

"No matter what is going on, the minute I board the ferry for the ride across the bay, my spirits soar and yet, it's hard to explain why."
−Scott Hirsch, 2023

Bear with me a few minutes; we will be in Fire Island quickly. I promise.

HOW DID I GET HERE?

I would like to say it all started right there, on that one mysteriously fateful Saturday afternoon in the locker room at East Islip High School or maybe that very same night in Ocean Beach.

It didn't.

In truth, it probably started well prior with my father's original decision to uproot, relocate and wrench me by the neck from my comfortable 'lifelong' Hicksville High School friendships to abruptly move us 'out east', and fast.

That decision, in the summer before my junior year of high school, was not greeted with a happy face. At the time, it was devastating.

I had spent countless hours playing three sports, becoming captain of the wrestling team and likely one of the youngest ever 9th graders to be called up to the high school to wrestle varsity.

More importantly, in the process, I had laid the foundation for, what I believed, were going to be lifelong friendships.

I had honed my lacrosse skills with endless hours of repetitive 'wall bouncing' to chalk-lined bricks and relentless STOP sign drills! Hitting S-T-O or P at will, like a bullet, from any angle or distance until the corner street light came on. I had put in my 10,000 hours, and it was just starting to pay off. I could feel the potential. It was everything to me.

I had become the starting goalkeeper of our soccer team just to stay in shape. I didn't even like soccer, but it fit my personal narrative to be the goalkeeper, the 'man'.

I had what I thought was a pretty hot little girlfriend, Gail McCormick (yes, a cheerleader…duh!).

Life was good, damn good. Amazingly good. I was respected in the junior high hallways of my little world. My bubble. Hell, I was the wingman to the school's number one 'stud', John Barberra. (In fact, Gail was his former babe, until she wasn't!).

Then the bubble burst.

Leaving this picture lane paradise never even occurred to me. Our street was literally called Picture Lane. Where I was becoming a bit of a young star player on its whiffle-ball concrete turf.

So, when it was summarily announced that we were moving, there was lots of screaming and crying. Plenty of tearful temper tantrums and *How-could-you-do-this-to-me's*.

We had to leave because a new street gang called the Pagans had taken up social residence on our Picture Lane corner. They had also apparently discovered that we were just about the only Jews in the whole neighborhood, and after a series of escalating incidents, my dad ended up in a wild confrontation on the front lawn involving his 22-caliber rifle. It was time to go, quickly.

Without even knowing it then, I had some lemonade to make from this early lemon. It would be finding Fire Island. A place I knew nothing about. No idea it existed. I would only find it because we had to move eastward.

There were other 'lemons', including my sweet mom's long ten-year battle with epilepsy stemming from a brain aneurysm at age thirty. Ironically, it would be a world-famous Fire Islander who would save her life, neurosurgeon Dr Joseph Epstein.

Perhaps these two 'things' set me on a certain path. Writing these stories is probably an attempt at a form of private therapy, with one small goal being to find some connection to my past.

The much larger goal, and my joy, is to share some one-of-a-kind stories I have been blessed to live through. Right here, on Baywalk. It's also a way to preserve the past and some unforgettable characters.

Things some have forgotten.

I promise we will shortly cross the Great South Bay together. Just a bit more on how it happened.

While we moved only 30 miles from Hicksville, Long Island, to the hamlet of East Islip, it might as well have been three hundred miles. If you are sixteen and don't drive on Long Island, you ain't going back to see your friends. With the limited and embarrassing exception of having to ask my dad to drive my Hicksville High crush, Gail, out to my East Islip homecoming dance and back, I never saw my old friends again. It's like they didn't really exist. It was sad enough that it still matters to me today. Even while I write this, it gnaws at me. *Just get over it, Scott.*

As I said, I will circle back to that contentious circumstance, leading to that temporary sadness and its related lifelong tensions with my father. Tensions that would probably stem from this sudden, jarring need to move the family. Tensions brought on, in my then childish mind, by his own overreactions to our becoming a target in the neighborhood. In my then mind, he made himself and, thus, our family a target of The Pagans. By discharging his 22-caliber rifle to fend off this gang on our front lawn, we had no choice. He had his reasons. I just refused to care or understand them.

For many years, I blamed my dad simply because he was a 'my way or the highway' guy. A child of the Depression, he saw the world in black and white. No nuances, no gray. Him against the world but with a glass half empty, take no risks modus operandi. It was easy to make him the scapegoat. He wasn't about to explain to me or anyone why this move was in our best interest. Parents didn't explain much of anything to their kids back then. Today, we probably would have been in group therapy for months. Back then, fathers made the decisions, and everyone followed.

No questions or comments from the peanut gallery.

Thankfully, as it turns out, you will see it leads to lots of great things, including the chance to find Fire Island. To tell this story of turning lemons into lemonade and earning my shot at paradise.

I guess I should thank my pop in heaven.

While he was alive, I certainly never thanked him. Just the opposite. I harbored anger and resentment for that move.

So, thanks Dad. It worked out just fine. I'm letting go of the anger. I think. I hope. I will try. It's a second chance.

I've had lots of second chances.

This is something I just now realized, just this second, while starting this book. As I look back, it's been a regular, recurring part of my life, through two high schools, two colleges, two law schools and two marriages. In hindsight, a clear pattern has emerged. Maybe two is my number! Second chances.

I set off on this personal journey to explore my life just by putting pen to paper. To make some sense of the randomness and perhaps find a common stitch. I think this book might just be about what I never expected. The continuous series of opportunities, often borne from 'crisis', that I have been fortunate enough to navigate, often never realizing it was happening and just charging forward. Each one, quietly making me stronger. Perhaps, the universe has been speaking this all along, and I just got lucky?

Wow, it's only the first chapter, and I have a revelation! I think I'll keep writing. This is cathartic. Let's see where it goes. I so hope you'll follow.

Let's have some fun.

Fire Island – Paradise Earned

A New School

We relocated in June, preceding my junior year.

The new school year had not yet started, but the chance to make new friends had. Summer soccer practice put me just outside but within the mix of the 'cool kids', the jocks who absolutely dominated life's social fabric (along with the football guys) at East Islip High School.

A 'new kid' thrown into the locker room of any testosterone-filled high school is going to feel some rights of passage, especially if you are the only Jew! I was no exception. Pretty quickly, I became a fun soft target.

"Hey Hicksville, who the F you think you are…you come here to steal a spot on our team?" "Hey, hook-nosed Jew bastard, where's your yarmulke?" (And these would become some of my closest friends, even until today, and we laugh about it!).

It's just what happens in high school. You take some sharp elbows to become accepted. No 'wokeism' here. None needed. It's just life. It's a good thing.

But after a while, keeping my head down, showing prowess on the field and taking some shrapnel, I was accepted by the jocks, and that (as any kid will tell ya) came with some perks.

Finding Fire Island

Less than a month into summer workouts, I was in the locker room.

"Hicksville, tell your parents you are sleeping over at Phil's house," exhorted one of my newly minted buddies. He added, "We are going to sleep in Fire Island tonight."

I quickly shot back, "Fire Island!? What the hell is that?" (I probably said fuck)

Swiftly came the reply, "Dickhead, don't ask too many questions. We are going over to Atlantique; we do it all the time – you'll love it. Just tell your parents you are sleeping out."

Still not sure, I replied, "But where do we sleep?"

Now the locker room boys were all listening.

"More questions, Hicksville? Look, we sleep under a guy's house. Don't worry, and no more questions."

(Not realizing I would someday be a lawyer) I couldn't stop. "Under a house – how is that possible?"

The group was getting more terse and tense now.

"Okay – last question, douchebag. The houses over there are built on stilts, so they are raised in the air. We sleep under the house! Don't be a pussy."

Now, when you are almost in eleventh grade, and a guy says that, with seven other guys behind him, and you want to be accepted, you shut the fuck up. That's exactly what I did.

And so it began. My first night in Fire Island. A night that would change my life forever. A night that would lead to the next chance to turn lemons into lemonade. A night that would fill all the other nights of my life and bring me so much joy. But first, I would have to earn it.

Get a Job

In a few short hours, we were a dozen boys and one girl riding across the Great South Bay, all crammed into one small boat. I don't think I had ever even been in a private boat before then. Certainly, never on this bay.

On the twenty-plus minute ride across the bay, the salty air filled my nostrils, and the wind on my face felt fantastic. It felt like…freedom and mystery. It seemed like it was pulling me.

Then, as the boat slowed and we neared the Fire Island shore, the rain began. No one seemed to care, but we did have to look for shelter. Lo and behold, the veteran travelers in the group easily directed the gang to a nearby house with ample space underneath to camp out. We piled under its imposing structure. I was in awe of our situation, thinking to myself, *did we really just take a half-hour ride for this?* Yet, it was strangely very cool, and I certainly wasn't asking any more questions.

At some point, as I now know it often does, the pre-summer rain just stopped. The Fire Island sky began to glow. Things started to happen. The group became restless and mobile.

On someone's silent signal, we made our way by foot through the sand, slurping cheap beers, Mad Dog 20/20 or Tyrolia wine. We were walking into the action zone, the intended target of our throbbing adolescent hearts, Ocean Beach.

The trip across the bay (my first ever) had been disorienting enough. I had never once been to The Great South Bay. Now, I was about to enter 'Oz'.

Ocean Beach, or 'OB', as I learned, was another level for me, a sixteen-year-old, with all its sights and sounds. So, it was like Oz.

Disco was just starting to move up with sharp elbows and slowly strangle my precious rock 'n' roll. My Springsteen, Eagles and Stones were being pushed aside by Abba, Dancing Queen, Donna Summer and Earth, Wind and Fire. The sexuality of that beat and all that went with it was now right in front of me.

The Saturday evening vibe had started, and it most definitely had a 'pulse'. Almost instantly, I loved it. I barely knew where we were on a map, but it didn't matter. In fact, that fact made it even better. It felt mysteriously dangerous, delicious and different. 'We are not in Kansas anymore', was the saying.

As the darkness on the edge of town gave way to shining disco lights, we split up into much smaller groups so as not to be too noticeable. One quick lap around the town to get my bearings. Then, by the time I walked into Town Pizza, I was hooked.

For the 'uninitiated', Town Pizza is exactly what it sounds like. The town's forever pizza parlor, smack in the middle of town. Only about twelve seats but lines out the door much of the time, and for a good reason. It had all the sights and sounds of a well-oiled machine with handsome blue-collar pizza boys and decked-out disco kids queuing up for a delicious slice of the cheapest, life-affirming meal in town. I still get excited now, almost 50 years later, for one of those slices with some extra cold cheese or Boom Boom on top (They know I like it 'room temp!'). Gotta be room temp. #townpizzaob #sideslicealley.

Plus, as I would come to find out, you stood a pretty good chance of 'hooking up' just by waiting in that line. This was the pre-1980s, pre-Aids, and these people knew how to party (as I would find out soon enough, and you will see).

Somehow, one of my buddies and I wound up in a conversation with the owner. Midway through the back and forth and some secret sips of our smuggled Seagram's Seven, I impulsively bleeped out, "Can I have a job here this summer?" It just popped out of my mouth.

Shockingly, the older Italian guy replied, "You seem like a nice kid; call me in aboutta week."

The next day, I called him (A pay phone, by the way).

Sounding stunned, and with a not-so-subtle Brooklyn accent, he says, "Didn't I tell you to wait abouttta week?"

"Yes sir, but I really want the job!"

With a very kind but stern Italian tint, he says, "I like you, kid; you should pack a bag and come over.

You gottajob." He didn't know I was still in Fire Island.

And so began my forty-four-year journey on our sandy barrier beach island. The one that has allowed me to turn lemons into lemonade time and time again. The place I call home and the one that still makes my heart beat faster.

All Work/No Play

The stories I am about to tell you are all true.

I promised myself that, if I was going to take massive time and emotional energy to put this on paper and out into the world, it could only be done this way. Genuinely really hoping (but not fully caring) you like it; makes it easy to be truthful.

And so it begins.

That summer of my pre-junior year in high school was filled with one thing – work (except for one very fateful night you'll see just below).

I was taught by the best how to make pizza, make dough, deal with customers, use a cash register, really truly clean, scrub and scrape an oven and work long hours. A typical work week was 75-80 plus hours. There was no such thing as overtime.

The guy in charge was a no-nonsense pro, hardened most likely by a career of pizza making in Brooklyn and New York City. I am ninety-nine percent sure his name was John, Pizza John. Or it could have been Eddie. I won't soon forget his redheaded girlfriend, though there's no way I can remember her name. I will have to ask Angelo, who still owns the joint. At age seventeen, he and I were teenage bunkmates in the back room. We are both still right where we belong.

I was bunking in the back room with the family that still owns it to this very day, though Angelo and I were just kids, his brother Carlo even younger.

The job came with 'free room and all the pizza you could eat'. We had our fun, don't get me wrong, but it usually consisted of quietly poking fun at the steady stream of disco ducks lining up late at night.

The pizza boys also loved the fabulous array of non-stop twenty-two-year-olds, with barely covered torsos, taking a break from the nearby sweaty dance floor (a place I would very soon happily wind up). We were seventeen, and that's what seventeen-year-old pizza boys do, even while covered in white flecks of flour. They still do. The pizza and girls are why you take the job.

Other than that, all I did was work 15-18 hours a day, 6-7 days a week. I was focused on one goal. To save up enough money to buy myself a highly coveted sound system. I'm talking about a setup I could someday soon take off to a college dorm.

We are talking about a Technics turntable, a Marantz amplifier, a Harmon Cardon receiver and JBL speakers! That was the prize. My goal. All work and no play. Make the money, and buy that sound system. I probably talked about it non-stop.

Until one night…

The Pixie Haired Blonde

Over the course of the summer, there was one young woman who was a regular that caught my eye. She was remarkably friendly and, as the kids now say, cute AF.

I would be lying if I told you I remember her name. I can tell you that she was a tiny pixie-haired blonde who looked like a 'cross between a yoga instructor and a biker chic' and that she was a DJ for a well-known Long Island radio station called WLIR. At the time, I had no idea she was about to change my life but in the weirdest way possible.

I can tell this story now, only because the statute of limitations on embarrassment has clearly expired.

After seeing her, and, I guess, flirting with her a half dozen times, I finally got the balls to ask her out. She was clearly older than me, as she looked about twenty-two. I think because she looked like a wild, free spirit, I thought, *hey, maybe I've got a chance.* This young alpha male rolled the dice.

To my sheer amazement, she agreed to go out with me! Now, in this very moment, this singular moment, Ocean Beach had me wrapped around its sexy little finger. This was a big deal.

As I said, this was 1976, and we were in Fire Island, one of two epicenters for the disco lifestyle and 'free love' on Fire Island (the other one being The Pines/Grove). If you were going out on any kind of a date, the chances were good that you were going to 'get down' as was the pop culture saying at the time.

I don't remember much, though we did get into The Apple Orchard and, I think, Dashers (For those familiar with Fire Island, they are now The Sandbar and Landing, respectively, and they both will play very heavily in my life, and this story going forward).

We did some sweaty, sexy dancing and just a bit more before the night was over.

The next morning, I woke up feeling crazy itchy all over, but mostly in my most private of areas. Throughout the morning, it became worse, and I started to freak out and get really concerned. I had never lived on my own, had no clue what this was, and I wasn't about to ask my 'bro coworkers'.

I dashed out front to Baywalk to look around for one of the older reliable party guys I could trust. That's where I found 'Frankie Frosted', as his closest friends called him.

Before I tell you the whole story, you gotta please let me tell you about Frankie.

Frankie was a gem, though a rather unusual one, even for the kinetic disco world of Ocean Beach. He was a crazy, young, handsome mix of John Travolta and The Fonz, but with a wisp of frosted hair over his masculine forehead. Dripping with sexuality, girls lined up just to sit next to him on the bench, his bench. He was always in the company of a gorgeous lady or two.

But, here's the strange part.

Frankie had taken some sort of a vague vow of silence. I'm not kidding. It was the ultimate 'shtick'. He could talk, but he wouldn't talk. I knew this because I had 'taken his pizza order' many times, and he would just smile and point. He was literally so fucking good-looking; he only had to point. He would never, ever answer a question. His sparkling eyes, his hands and his gestures did all his talking. And the girls loved it. Kinda like how The Fonz just punched the jukebox, and it played, and then how he would snap his fingers, and gals would faint into his arms. That was Frankie. Frankie Frosted.

I ran outside and there he was, on his bench. I ran towards him.

Not expecting a verbal answer, I shouted, "Hey Frankie, can I talk to you?

I was frantic, still scratching myself while he was looking me over and already making knowing faces up at me. That damn sexy smirk already showing.

"Frankie, I don't know what's going on, but I'm miserable and I can't stop scratching!" As he looked me over, I continued. "I went out with this girl last night (his eyes now popping open), and I had my first good night here and now this. What do I do?"

With that, Frankie's smirk became a chuckle, then a laugh. He rolled his eyes and got off the bench, simultaneously motioning me to follow him. No words. We walked three blocks down the street to Milt Goodman's drugstore (It's now the Sweet Castle Ice Cream Shop).

Frankie strutted in, and Milt greeted him (not expecting any verbal hello or reply). Frankie pointed up to the shelf. Milt took down a small white box and handed it to Frankie, who handed it to me. Frankie made some kind of polite 'monkey-like' hand gestures while I tried to read the box.

Frankie was smirking now with that handsome face of his, like a proud dad showing his kid the ropes. I got it. Now I understand!

I paid, and Frankie walked me back to his bench. I thanked him. Obviously, no reply. He was still grinning as I pivoted away, back to shower in my little room with the contents of the little white box.

About two days later, I was feeling better. I was relieved and back to just keeping my head down and doing nothing but work. It was August. I was hot. I hoped I didn't see the pixie-haired girl. The tiny pizza joint was hot and sticky, and my only night off ended in complete disaster.

So, I was done. I was finished. I made up my mind that I was leaving Fire Island after Labor Day, about two to three weeks away at this point. I started to mumble openly at work about my unhappiness. I started to say, "I'm one and done." I wasn't hiding it. It was over for me. No more Fire Island. No more thoughts about buying the sound system. Just trying to plow through and honor my commitment until I went back to school.

About a week or so later, at about 8 pm, the boss John came up to me. He tapped my shoulder and said, "I want to see you out in the alley." (Note: The Sopranos didn't exist yet).

At this point, it's worth letting you know that, in today's terms, this would be like 'Pauli Walnuts' grabbing your arm and saying, *let's take a walk*. It was quite unsettling.

The alley back then isn't what it is today. Today, it's got some seats and nice fences. Then, it was where we stored the garbage, and it was getting dark. Naturally, I was thinking, *this can't be good*. I don't know; maybe the guy thought I was stealing from him? Worry came over me.

We stepped into the dim, dank, dark, smelly alley.

He stared at me and barked, "What's this I hear? You ain't coming back?"

Quickly, I thought, I can't tell him the 'crabs story'! It was way too embarrassing, and he was my boss. Plus, he'd tell his really hot girlfriend.

I shifted gears and stammered a reply, "Well, I'm just not happy and…" boom, he cut me right off!

He barked again, "Put out your hands," and started to move his hand towards his rear pocket.

Anxiously, I thought, *this guy definitely thinks I stole from him, and he's gonna whack me right there in the alley or at least give me a beat down*. But I do as he says. Sheepishly, I move my two open palms out toward him.

With that, he pulled out a stack of hundred-dollar bills. He counted off six or eight and pushed them into my hands, but he didn't let go. With his massively strong manly hands, he gripped my hands and the green cash in them at the same time.

Squeezing down, he said, "I want you to take this money and buy that fuckin music thing, that stereo; you been moaning bout all summah, but only on one condition."

I listened, my heart pounding between the relief of not getting beat up and the confusing feel of the crisp bills in my hand.

Forcefully again and pressing my hands even harder, he said, "The condition is, I don't wanna hear you not comin' back cause you're the best worker I ever seen, you hear me?"

And with that, not missing a beat, I gathered a smile and said, "I'll be back," to which he now pushed his index finger into my chest and said, "Good, now get back to work."

And so it goes, somehow lemons turned into lemonade, and life changed in an instant. My Fire Island journey would continue, at least for one more year.

Reflecting all these years later, I think, but for the pixie-haired blonde girl and getting bought in the 'side slice' alley, I would never have continued this journey. It was supposed to have ended with the summer of 1976. One and done.

Second chances.

Damn, I wish I could remember her name. Maybe she's on Facebook. Thank you, Ms. WLIR.

Onward & Upward

Over the next couple of years, life would take me through graduation and on to college, then law school, all while coming back to Ocean Beach each summer and steadily moving up the town work ladder.

During this time, I was becoming proximately closer to the orbits of key players in the downtown and the community and, I think, slowly earning their trust. Or, at least, I was becoming a familiar face who wasn't getting in trouble and staying a reliable worker. This evolution in paradise is that story.

My story.

This is probably a good place to make a quick observation about how Fire Island was really impacting my life, world view and personal trajectory. It was never easy to leave after the season and go back to school. The 'real world' just seemed mundane and boring. It seemed like a black-and-white movie, and I needed technicolor. One of the most satisfying elements of my nascent Fire Island life was the regular interactions with all manner of 'rascals and raconteurs'.

Many of these people went on to play hugely significant roles at critical junctures in my life. Mostly, they opened my eyes and mind to a wider world. A world full of travel and adventure, love and lust, food and wine, music, art, film and politics. In short, my Fire Island education was filling me with more useful knowledge, substance and sustenance than any school book could.

It literally molded the contours of my psyche. I owe 'her', 'the island' and all those mentors along the way quite a bit. That's why I now spend a good deal of time mentoring other young workers all the time and whenever I can. I will happily highlight many of those mentors throughout this story.

Speaking of those generous mentors, one in particular helped set in motion a direct sequence of events leading to many more chances at lemonade making. Her name was Arlene Jaffe.

Arlene was Ocean Beach's leading real estate broker, and she knew everyone. Even more than that, though, she was keenly generous of spirit and, if she liked you, she looked for ways to help you. She had a domineering presence and, in a time and place where men were the only sharks. She was having none of it.

She was a chainsmokin' 'broad' with a sharp tongue who loved to connect people with beach life and buy and sell their dream homes. Summers in Fire Island and winters in Acapulco, she was always tall and tan. She was the first female I had ever seen, making me understand that women could do anything a man could do and maybe better. This was the opposite of my home life, where my mom was a sweet but gentle, obedient homemaker.

A woman businessperson who was at the center of economic, political and social life in a whole town? It was a sight to behold. She moved the center of gravity for me in thinking about how women interacted with the world. Much later on, I would meet another such dynamic lady, Mayor Natalie Rodgers, a true inspiration. We'll get to that much later.

For reasons lacking importance and comprehension, Arlene took a liking to me. An actual interest in how my growing work life was progressing.

I first met her while working those two seasons at Town Pizza. When I returned for a third season, now nineteen, I was asked to bartend at her friend 'Billies' new place, called Fellas (This is now Taco Beach). I never knew if Arlene planted that one. It would not surprise me.

The First Steps on the Ladder

Billie was a hard-charging, no-nonsense lesbian who had opened up a bar with another local legend named Giovanni. Giovanni 'Gio' Palmieri owned CJs, the town's co-central watering hole and the only year-round bar. Billie already owned Billies, a luncheonette. Somehow, these two got together, opened this small bar restaurant and were staffing up. This was a very rare shot at a new, unstaffed place, so I jumped at the chance.

Having made the decision at the end of season two not to keep making summertime pizza for hourly wages, I would attempt to break into the world of tips and hospitality. It seemed to be closer to the action and really meeting people. Plus, I could start to make some real money. College, even at $7500 a year, plus the food was expensive.

Bartending gigs were super hard to get, and this was a new little place with no real staff yet. I had just enough experience with the basics from bartending at some freshman college parties. The world of 'fancy martinis and mocktails' had not begun. Basically, I white-lied my way into that first real job 'behind the stick'. I worked this third season at Fellas, and it was pretty unremarkable.

Anyway, that's where I got to know Arlene, who often came by Fellas in the evening to have a meal or cocktail with her friends Gio and Billie. This friendship would set in motion a series of events where each time she made the phone call magically furthered my trajectory and led me to where I am today. I am forever indebted to her.

The First Call

As I said earlier, the place to be back then, if you craved the action, was The Apple Orchard. It was owned by twin brothers, Herbie and Jack.

These guys were rebels and real 'nightclub types', who were constantly running into scrapes and trouble with the local police chief. I mean trouble, even to the point of rolling around in the street and getting cuffed. They were 'city boys', shaking things up at the beach. They wouldn't be the last, but to me, they were the first.

In 1979, this was truly the 'land of no', as it had properly been tagged repeatedly in the news at the time. Its Chief of Police was Joe Loeffler Sr., a no-nonsense, dedicated cop. So, running an uber-successful 'disco' or nightclub smack dab in the middle of town was always going to be a challenge.

Yet, they did it, only occasionally getting thrown in jail!

Should anyone think I am condoning wild, untamed, raucous fun at the expense of good common sense citizenry, I am not. No way. Threading that needle takes care and effort, something I know a lot about. For now, I am simply recalling events.

I liked my job at Fellas, but I was getting bored with its very limited seating and it being basically a lunch or dinner-and-done spot. I really wanted a job where the action was. The 'Orchard', as it was nicknamed, was the spot. I worked at Fellas and made pizza on the side for Mike the Greek (now Rachel's) that entire third summer. My heart was somewhere else, though.

Toward the end of that third season, I asked Arlene (somewhat rhetorically) if she knew the guys who owned the 'Orchard', as I was thinking of trying to land a spot there the following season. Well, she took this idea personally, and she wasn't going to let it die on the vine.

Shortly after mentioning the idea, one day, Arlene told me she spoke to Herbie, and he would try to find me 'something', though it might not be bartending. Apparently, his staff was all coming back, but he told her maybe I could become a barback until something opened up.

I didn't hesitate at the 'offer', knowing that I had to pay my dues and that the money would probably be equal to what I was seeing at Fellas. With that, Arlene arranged a short 'hello meeting', just before I went back off to college.

Somehow, I had lined up a job at the Orchard, the hottest spot in town, thanks to Arlene. It won't be the last time she would help me get the job that ultimately led to buying my own slice of Fire Island heaven.

A Word About College First

Not everyone goes to college, and certainly not everyone goes to law school. Even fewer wind up going to two colleges and two law schools. Since those stories have a great deal to do with events that (again) started with lemons, I have decided they merit some mentioning. Life was not all Fire Island all the time.

So, I have to go back in time just a little bit. But I will return to the Fire Island stuff right away. I promise.

When it was first decided that I would even go to college, the options were quite limited. Limited due to family finances and my lack of any great scholastic prowess. I was a half-decent student but an even less decent standardized test taker. My disappointing SAT profile further narrowed the options. My world, at that time, was playing lacrosse, a sport that was just beginning to take shape on Long Island. Unlike today, there were only a small number of excellent Long Island high schools that dominated the game. Most fabulous players were still from deep upstate New York or Maryland, though Long Island was also on their radar.

Looking back, one of the main reasons I was so angry at my dad for scurrying us away from Hicksville was that it was one of the few schools that had a deeply respected lax program. I was 'in line' to move up and make some moves that could have led to more college options.

Then 'boom', overnight, that chance was gone as my new school didn't even have a lacrosse program! None. It didn't exist. Football, yes – that was their game. They were Long Island Champs under the strong hand of the legendary Coach Sal Champi. Himself a legend, Champi's football teams would often win the prestigious Rutgers Cup Trophy. If you lived in East Islip, you didn't miss a football game. Football was life in our school.

When I found out there was no lacrosse, I was deeply angry. I wasn't having it. No way. These were some rotten lemons.

I went to Coach Champi's assistant coach, 'Doc' Holiday. Doc was also one of my teachers. I would have approached Mr. Champi, but like most of the school, I was petrified to talk to him or make eye contact. You didn't just start a conversation with Sal Champi. You might wind up doing 50 push-ups.

I approached Doc with a plan. Help me and the school build the next great team, and we will use the football players to keep them in off-season shape and knock people out of my way on the field. I figured he would eventually have to get Mr. Champi's blessing anyway, so why not include football guys during an opposing season of play. Doc agreed. The East Islip Lacrosse program was born, and I was its captain. More lemonade, I guess.

25

Today, 45 years later, that program is just superb and truly outstanding. One of the best in all of Long Island.

We did okay, and the football guys loved it. Now, they could 'lay people out' at full speed and with a stick in their hands! I got to keep my skills going and keep this sport fresh on future college applications. I wasn't ever getting recruited coming from a brand new program, but I would find a way forward.

By the second year (my senior year), we were actually pretty decent, and even Coach Champi took an interest in the sport, occasionally showing up when a game didn't conflict with his varsity baseball team's schedule. Just having Coach Champi on your sideline was electrifying (His baseball team was where I first met future NFL MVP Quarterback Boomer Esiason, our most famous alumni and still a friend). The fact that Coach might even see you in the locker room or hallway and say, "Hirsch, nice job out there yesterday," was like a sweet thunderbolt of satisfaction.

For me, the college landscape was now made up of the only two SUNY schools that would have me and who had excellent lacrosse programs, Cortland State and Stony Brook. It was a no-brainer. One was way too close to home with a mediocre lax team, and the other was just far enough away with a legendary team that would be difficult to 'walk on'. I chose the latter, Cortland State.

While it wasn't that difficult to get into the school, going to school and staying enrolled would turn into a huge challenge and yet another batch of lemons. Lemons created by *moi*.

The school had a well-deserved reputation for its students knowing how to party, especially among its athletes. I had some very serious lax skills by most standards, but the men who were there on 'full rides' were a whole different breed. Partiers, yes, but with athleticism and stamina, I had rarely seen. It was pretty obvious that, though I somehow made the team as a walk-on, I would see very little, if any, playing time.

Still, what an honor to play amongst some of the best the game has ever produced. Two guys on the attack line ahead of me were multi-year, All American selections. If anyone ever had the chance to see Mark 'KP' Koetzner or Mike Hoppy play the sport, they would surely understand.

We played and practiced hard and then partied just as hard almost at the same time. I've told my own kids this story as a cautionary tale, but at one time, I saw the sunrise fifteen nights in a row. The net result was a predictable GPA that had me hanging by much less than a thread. Probation is the nicest word for it. A gloriously shameful 1.77 average. On the bright side, I got to see a UFO.

One day, and I am not sure how, I just decided that I had to get out of there. It wasn't working.

Somewhere, deep down in my soul, I knew I had to leave. I remember going to the giant pay phone in the hallway and calling my parents.

Nervously, I dialed home.

"Mom, Dad, don't get concerned, but I have to find a new school. I can't go into detail, and I'm okay, but staying here won't be good for me or my future."

I don't recall the responses, but I'm sure they asked lots of questions.

The problem was that (as I soon realized) no one wanted me. No decent school would take a second-string lax player with a 1.77 GPA. Other schools each basically said, "Stay where you are and show us two back-to-back semesters of 3.40 or better, and we might realistically take you as a transfer student." At a minimum, that now meant coming back as a sophomore.

With that, I made a promise to myself to stop smoking pot with my lax buddies and teammates and actually attend classes. My sophomore year would be different. I wanted more from life. Time to squeeze the lemons. I just had to do better. I wanted a second chance.

I stopped smoking dope, put in the effort and hit the goal. A 3.40 and 3.60 GPA during my sophomore semesters would lead to my being accepted as a transfer student to Rutgers University (though not Rutgers College). Rutgers had a very serious D1 lacrosse team as well. However, this time, all three guys on the attack-men line ahead of me were multi-year All-Americans! But first, it's back to Fire Island.

Back to the Beach

Things were about to tick up a notch for me with this dramatic entrance into the world of disco and a job at the hottest club in western Fire Island. The year was 1980, and come September, I would be transferring to Rutgers with the hope of getting a walk-on spot in a very serious lacrosse program. But first, it was a summer of paying my dues as the 'ice boy' at The Orchard, the center of the western Fire Island dance club universe at the time.

I have far too many crazy stories to share about my time at The Orchard, some of which are even too 'naughty' to commit to print. Some things I saw and things I occasionally did must be left for private, small group conversation. As you might understand, they almost always included booze, sex and coke or, in those days, more likely quaaludes!

Since the job came with a bed upstairs, it was not at all unusual to take a well-timed 'break' in the middle of a song for a completely spontaneous distraction of one kind or another. Sometimes, it might be right on the stairs on the way up, unable to wait for the ten extra steps!

You knew how much time you had based on where the song was hitting. When Ricky Rella lit up Sugar Hill Gang's brand new 7-minute song, 'Rappers Delight', all bets were off. Hip hop hippity hop, you don't stop. Plenty of time to play.

One of my favorite memories was bunking with legendary DJ Ricky Rella. It's where I got my fascination with dance music and what it could do in the hands of a true master. It was an actual thrill to carry his records (yes, only Vinyl) for him. Ricky was the house music man at The Orchard. One of the only players who used three turntables, not two.

He would work up some sweat in the booth and, with just his mixes and song choices, cause some wild activities to burst out on the floor. Occasionally, in those days, even some fellatio.

He lived to share new music drops that obviously didn't just show up on Spotify or SoundCloud. In those days, he had to go find them. He had to hit the Bronx and Brooklyn street corners! Then test them out on the hottest dance floor outside of Studio 54, where he was also known to play. Bunking with him meant I could get an advance sneak peek at some new artists before they went big time. It was not unusual to have record companies try to get Ricky to break out a new release in Fire Island even before the radio. These were heady days in the disco landscape, and by accident and luck, I was rooming with one of the top DJs in the country. Wow.

The Orchard had a friendly rivalry with another club, a newer club called Dashers. Dashers was owned by some mobbed-up characters, Chicky and Dennis. They had a small illegal casino upstairs.

Luckily for me, if you worked at The Orchard, you didn't wait in line at Dashers and vice versa. It was at Dashers where I realized there was a kind of female, a 'girl' who could bring a room to a silent stop just by entering. I tell this story not because of any closeness to that person. I tell it because it's where I learned the subliminal lesson that 'who is serving the drinks matters'.

I had never before seen beauty used as a weapon up close. A stun gun, made of grace, charm, and sexuality perceived as so accessible, so powerful, it made men forget where they were or what they were spending. That was the lesson.

Thank you, Kathy Angel (I think Angel might have been a fake name). Just the fact that we almost never spoke, and I remember your name 40 years later, says it all. In the theatre of hospitality, always have an Angel.

Dashers was also the place I met another wickedly talented DJ, Jim Gaffey. Jim quietly taught me an interesting lesson that he didn't even know. He taught me that not everyone in the bar business is destined for a life of divorce and or debauchery. Jim was with Iris and still is. Both were in their early twenties; they were as young as me. The two of them were inseparable and still are today.

It gives me immense pleasure to this day when Jim pops into my club with Iris and their daughter Mikaila for a round of late-night dancing. It's a bond and link for me back to a time and place where I was soaking up the scene like a young sponge. Jim reminds me we are never too old to dance!

Don't Take Your Shirt Off

My first trip outside Ocean Beach was to the true land of Oz, the Fire Island Pines. I'm not sure why we remember some things, but on this one, I'm pretty sure. It happened that summer.

The Fire Island Pines, locally just called The Pines, is one of two gay communities on Fire Island. It has a unique and wholly different vibe than any other community. At that time, the vibrant colors of the daytime gave way to nightly, carnival-like versions of Studio 54 meets Cirque Du Soliel.

I was a 21-year-old, heterosexual boy, safely ensconced in my masculinity, but also very curious from all the wild chatter about 'The Pines'. While only working five miles away in Ocean Beach, the chatter contained constant references to 'The Land of Oz'.

So, when a local Ocean Beach regular asked if I wanted to go to a party in The Pines, I jumped at the chance. My invite at the time came from a lady married to one of Long Island's most infamous bar owners, and they were constantly in the news. The Mathesons had a formula racing boat that could rocket us down the six-mile bayfront trip in minutes. They called these boats 'Fountains', maybe because of the fountains of water they displaced in their wake.

As we jumped in the boat to leave the dock, our host Carolyn pulled me aside to whisper in my ear.

"Only one rule, Scott; don't take off your shirt when we get there." She further explained that it would mean I was 'available and interested'. I smiled and thanked her.

About 4-5 minutes later, we slowed down to enter the Land of Oz. Engines cut, we slowly glided into the mouth of the gorgeous marina and it's welcoming harbor. Around the harbor, music from the clubs formed the pulsing background, and the foreground was taken up by massively magnificent homes, large yachts and colorful shops.

Over the pulse of the slowing engines, it was announced that our destination was the house on the bay just to our left. As we glided into the harbor, we could see the steady stream of barely clad men (and a few women) walking around the marina boardwalks toward the bayfront mansion. The boat was docked, and off we went. We were now in Oz.

As we neared the home and its private entrance just off the marina, the bodies and their motion came into closer focus and view. This was a house party unlike anything I'd ever seen. The landscaping and lighting along the bay were as breathtaking as the guests. I didn't know where to look first. All I knew was that this was nothing like Ocean Beach.

With the bay on my left, I was less than 30 feet inside the compound. To my right, I saw a picnic table occupied by a dozen guests and a large mound of white powder on top. There were already lines to do lines.

Swiveling my head back to the left and toward the bay, a band was in full swing, and dancers were three deep. Taking a half dozen more steps, I looked up and to my right. There, on the rooftop, was a DJ spinning music with the moon just over his shoulder. The house was rocking. The music from the bars back inside the marina was now a distant hum. The party was here. Lights, color, sound, motion, beauty and laughter were what I observed. I was happy.

After I went inside, I realized I had to actually use the bathroom. I asked one of the guests if they knew where it was. The mustached man in all white linen pointed to a sleek staircase off to the side of the room. Off I went to relieve myself and then start the night.

Finishing the climb, I walked through the hallway, passing artwork like I had only ever seen in magazines. I recall one or two pieces saying 'Lichtenstein'. It felt like vibrant pop art.

I toggled one or two doors that didn't open and finally landed on one that did.

As I turned the handle and pried open the door, I was met with a one-of-a-kind show I had never seen before, or even since; an orgy.

It's not a memory you easily forget. A full-blown orgy, like something you would see in a movie only after you show your ID.

When I started writing this story, I wasn't sure if I would include this anecdote. I started to think about why I should or shouldn't. Did it really say anything? Why would it matter?

I came to the realization that, somehow that night was very important to me. It literally stood out all these years. The details are still so vivid and rich in my head that I feel it must have meant something after so many years. After careful reflection, here is all I can say about that.

While I closed the door quickly after opening it, I will not deny lingering for more than a split second. I had zero interest in participating, but I must have been so enthralled at the momentary voyeuristic experience that it stayed with me as if it were yesterday. It sent a jarring signal to my young brain that not everyone lives a 'Leave it to Beaver' lifestyle and that maybe even 'Mr. Beaver (Ward Cleaver) secretly enjoys crossing the lines now and again'.

Life is not monochromatic. It's a rainbow of colors. Be open to adventure.

Quite powerfully, it said to me, "There is much more than one way to live your life, and don't forget that." Live your life the way you want. I think my continuous support for and empathy and connection with those who have chosen other lifestyles might have begun that night. It is impossible to say.

That's why including the story makes sense here. It's another reason why I owe Fire Island so much. Visiting The Pines and its sister community, The Grove, each summer is still a special day or night for me. I try to connect many of our guests with a trip there whenever I can. It can be life-changing. I think it was for me.

The Apple Orchard

As this was my fourth season at the beach and my first season working at The Orchard, I was intent on proving myself to the older guys. Ice boys don't become bartenders by accident. You gotta earn it.

Threading the needle between keeping your head down, staying out of the way, and yet always being where you are needed is not simple. It's something we still teach young staff. It's like watching a ballgame and seeing the guys without the ball constantly moving. It's another reason why I try to hire athletes. At the same time, I had some ideas about getting noticed.

The main bartenders were two older guys I am very proud to say I am still friends with, Andy Miller and Steve Cummings. Andy and Steve have been quiet mentors of mine for decades. Standup guys who have made blessed and outstanding lives and careers for themselves and their families both on and off the beach. Andy lives year-round in Ocean Beach, and Steve lives year-round in Ocean Beach, California.

Having said that, I know they were not thrilled with my idea of getting some attention while working in the chaotic disco Mecca, that was The Orchard. I was their ice boy, but I had 'The Whistle'.

Getting through the thick crowds to stock a busy bar and have some fun required the occasional 'toot toot, beep beep, whistle pop' to the beat of the music and made some kind of crazy impression. Moderation was the key. I would just have to be cool and not blow it near Andy and Steve. Otherwise, I don't care what they now say; it was a hit, I think.

The great thing about places like The Apple Orchard is that if you hustle and earn respect, the older guys will show you the ropes and pass the torch. That's what these guys did for me. By the time August came, having shown me how it's done, they would let me pour drinks when they went on a 'bathroom break'.

Since those bathroom breaks could last 5-10 minutes those days, that was all I needed. That's where I started to meet everyone who would later play a central role in making my dream come true. I met them in the 'hot corner'. The end of the L-shaped bar, where they all hung out and had 'reserved space' and quick, first-look drinks waiting for them. Their glasses were never empty.

Andy and Steve gave me just enough space and warm welcome intros to pry open the doors and help make that happen. For that and their lifelong mentoring, I am forever grateful.

Many years later, I would go on to become one of the youngest trustees elected in our little beachside Village and proudly take a seat next to Andy in the process.

Working with him and others was a great experience. But we will get to that later. For now, we return to 'The Orchard' and then off to Rutgers and The Scarlet Knights.

Love and Lust on Fire Island

It's no secret and certainly not rocket science to figure out that one of the more significant and compelling migrations toward the summer sea and beach life is the hope of finding either love, lust, or both. When you take the salty passion, mix in a bit of Tequila, and strike up the music and freedom friction, sparks can and do fly. Sometimes those summer sparks turn into fall fantasy and then winter wonderlands. Every once in a while, they turn into full-blown lifetime love affairs.

I have had all three.

The Island has given me three such richly memorable connections. One tumultuous and fairly brief, providing a much-needed chance to actually grow up. One moderately short and remarkably painful.

The last, thankfully, was, and still is, very long and allowed me the best journey I could have ever asked for.

As I said, this effort is not worth doing unless it bears truthful witness to my life and its related adventures, both painful and joyous.

As we all know, quite often, these romances happen at work. The restaurant/nightclub scene is epic for its prowess and production of romantic opportunities.

This was the case for coming face to face with my first serious girlfriend. I had been blessed with some fabulous high school girlfriends. Really, amazing people who I probably didn't deserve. But living with someone is a whole different level.

While working at The Orchard, I began a relationship with Denise F. She was a cocktail waitress and a little bit older than me. Confident, brash, sexy and all unfiltered truth all the time. She was a Hauppauge girl and was way more schooled in the world than me. She was in charge of her life and most of mine for a time. And I liked it. It wasn't healthy, but I liked it. The stronger and more domineering women were much more attractive to me at that moment in time. I was along for the ride. It was a wild ride, and I was all in.

I don't recall all the details as time fades many memories, but she was the first person with whom I ever took a plane and a trip, let alone lived with. You don't forget that, and certainly not with Denise. After the summer, but before returning to college, we packed bags and went from San Francisco to Ensenada Beach in Mexico. The whole coast. She was my tour guide, and together, I got my first taste of the west coast, a larger planet, and what it was like to ride a stallion, both literally and figuratively. At times, exhilarating and emasculating, but never ever dull.

I am grateful to her for all of that and more. Though only a bit older, "Here's to you, Mrs. Robinson."

There came a time, a short couple years later, when I had to make a decision that would change things in a difficult way. When I graduated college, I was heading off to Chicago for law school, and that put the final nail in the box that had become a very tempestuous relationship. It was one of those 'it's me or you' moments. I chose me.

I know now that I got it absolutely right. Looking back allows the fog of love to clear. At the time, I remember it being difficult to breathe. I was not the first person to 'abandon' her, and it was loud and raw.

On the Banks of the Raritan

The Raritan River runs through New Brunswick, New Jersey, home of Rutgers University. Rutgers is made up of five colleges and is home to The Scarlet Knights.

Somehow, through sheer force of will and grit, digging deep into my storage of desire for a better life, I made the jump from SUNY Cortland and my fucked up 1.77 GPA to Livingston College at Rutgers

University. Honestly, I'm not even sure how I pulled off getting a 3.4 and 3.6 back-to-back semesters at Cortland to generate the single stat needed to transfer. Somehow, I did.

All the Rutgers colleges shared the campus. So, I was officially a Scarlet Knight. I had a chance, a very slim one, to play some division 1 lacrosse in the process.

But first, I had to figure out where to live.

Phi Gamma Delta

It gets interesting here because I took a step into something as a leap of faith that was not normal.

My older brother had graduated from Rutgers College, and during his tenure there, had become an outstanding member of one of its oldest fraternities, Phi Gamma Delta, or 'FIJI' as it's known all over the country. Becoming a FIJI brother would be a big deal at Rutgers. This led to the rare and maybe unprecedented idea of living IN the fraternity house while still actually pledging it.

In hindsight, that was probably an insane idea. Pledging a fraternity is stressful enough. Living in the fraternity at the same time makes you available 24/7 for shenanigans of all kinds. On top of that, someone decided, "Let's put the rookie junior year pledge in the same room as the two oldest, rowdiest brothers in the entire house!" These guys were on the 7-year college plan, and I was their little mascot slave for quite a while. They made Bluto from Animal House seem like a pet hamster.

Somehow, despite the ritualistic hazing under such hilarious names as 'snack fuck' and the pillow cases of dog poop, I made it. I was, and will forever be, a FIJI brother. Any FIJIs out there, hit me up for the secret handshake.

Along the way, two things happened that stand out as turning points in my trajectory.

First, when I saw how poorly I had done in my core science classes at Cortland State, I abandoned my foolish plans of becoming a veterinarian. Vet school acceptance was harder to achieve than med school at that time. So, I pivoted to thinking about following my brother and a law degree. In that process, upon transfer, I changed my studies to Labor Relations, which was a bit of a premier major at my new school and a good fit for a possible law career. As it turned out, my campus had a very well-regarded but newly formed Labor Relations Major program. For the first time, I began to enjoy school and learning.

The Scarlet Knights

Although the chances of playing on any D1 sports program as a walk-on are really slim, I couldn't just give up on that dream. I was way too invested in my 10,000 hours and my passion for lacrosse. I knew from my experience at Cortland, a D2 school, just how hard it was, and this was at least a level up. Just making the roster, without getting any playing time, would be a true achievement.

To make matters even more difficult, this team had not one, not two, but three All-American attackmen ready to go. Plus, a fourth that was fabulous in every way. If I was lucky, I might make the 5th slot and almost never play. It didn't stop me.

Tom Sweeney, Bobby Olsen and Jimmy Ford (or as the sportscasters would often say, 'Sweeney to Olsen to Ford, shot and score') were so good it was like they were one person. All groomed from big-time Long Island programs, they were faster, tougher, and quicker than almost anyone I had ever played with or competed against.

It was an eye-opener in the sense that my bubble burst, and I learned a valuable set of lessons. Not the least of which was there is always someone hungrier and better than you, so you have to outwork them to even have a chance.

I survived. I made the cut. I got to play with some of the most talented and fiercely competitive guys to ever hold a stick. Legends to this day. I also got to travel to some amazing campuses. Army, Navy, Cornell, Hopkins, Princeton, and Virginia, to name just a few. These experiences further forged my view of what was 'out there'. Lacrosse was great, but it was just a vehicle for seeing more of the country and life outside of Suffolk County, New York.

With my Labor Relations classes going well, my FIJI pledging done, and my lacrosse world somewhat still intact, it was time to return to my happy place, my 'home' – Fire Island.

It would start to get really interesting from then on.

Moving Further up the Ladder

While I was working at The Apple Orchard the year before, I had heard a rumor that the place down the street, the place called Leo's, might be looking for a day bartender.

Just to fast forward for a second, Leo's was now the Island Mermaid. But as you will see, there was going to be about nine years until that was to happen. In between, there were a lot of stories to tell. This trip is far from a straight line. I hope you'll stay with me.

At this point, the 'grande dame', Arlene Jaffe, again played a pivotal role.

I reached out to her.

"Arlene, I could use a favor. I heard there might be an opening at Leo's for a day bartender, and I hear the Apple Orchard is up for sale; do you know the guy Leo who owns Leo's?"

It was a rhetorical question. I had seen Arlene with Leo in town many times and at The Orchard more than once.

"Of course, I sold him his house! You want me to get you an interview?" Forever my champion.

"Arlene, that would be amazing. I hear the place is busy, and I know a lot of the customers already." (It's a small town, so these people all hung out at Leo's for sunsets and happy hour and the evening hit The Orchard until late at night).

Within days, I had an apportionment to go meet Mr. Leo Schumer in New York City. Wow. I was nervous, excited, and more than a bit out of my league at the time.

To me, here is where the fun parts begin.

Leo

First, let me please tell you about Leo. As a kind of New York celebrity, he was known everywhere as just 'Leo'.

The easiest way to describe him would be to say, "Think foul-mouthed, Jewish Danny Devito," for starters.

By trade, he was hardly a restauranteur and more of a raconteur! He was a very well-respected 'Madison Avenue' piano jingle writer who happened to own a very popular watering hole and eatery. I am reliably told he wrote such famous jingles as 'Plop plop fizz fizz' for Alka Seltzer and 'Let Your Fingers Do the Walking' for Yellow Pages. His connections to the TV, advertising, and show business world didn't hurt his restaurant business. His Manhattan life and home were what you would expect; elegant and prime.

Through his assistant, I made the appointment to be interviewed by him at his home on Fifth Avenue, in what could be described as The Jackie Kennedy Onassis building overlooking Central Park. What I didn't know was that the entire interview would last about 30 seconds.

Nervously, I put on my best (and maybe only) Searsucker Suit and tie and boarded the train from East Islip, Long Island, to Manhattan. If I recall, it was my first trip to NYC. Certainly, it was my first one alone.

On the train ride, I ran scenarios in my head as to what he might ask. I knew he was a sarcastic, edgy guy who might take well to a certain kind of swagger. I had some answers to make-believe questions illuminated in my mind during the hour-plus train ride.

I approached the magnificent building, trying to relax and slow down. Greeted by the doorman first and then the houseman, I was told to take a seat in front of (what else) the grand piano. Just behind the piano was Central Park. It was magnificent. I was as nervous as ever, and then I noticed the piano seemed to be playing itself.

The music stopped, and only then did I realize that Leo was playing the piano, but I could barely see him (remember, I said Danny Devito).

A raspy voice boomed from the piano seat. The piano was now silent.

"So, my friend Arlene says you are a great fucking worker, but why should I hire you?"

Now, luckily having thought about just this kind of question on the train ride, I didn't hesitate or miss a beat. Not 2 seconds.

In my most sincere but cocky voice, I snapped back, "Because, Mr. Schumer, someday I'm gonna own that place, and I gotta know what to do!"

With that, he laughed and said, "You're hired, kid. Now get the fuck outta here!"

Interview over. Classic Leo. My head was spinning.

And so, after only a few years in the trenches, the main part of my 46-year Fire Island journey, with all its magical branches, began. I was now the day bartender at Leo's Place. Again, thanks to Ms. Jaffe, #badassbitch.

Sadly, I got to work only one season for Leo.

Incredibly, over the following winter, he didn't survive an open heart surgery. Thus, the next chapter (still in the same building) was about to begin. The building in which Island Mermaid would be born.

After that season, one more return to Rutgers for my senior year and then the LSATs as I had decided (again) to follow my brother and pursue a law career.

Wally's Place

The Island Mermaid building has been four things in its lifetime. I have started here with number two, Leo's Place.

I will happily return later here for some one of a kind stories about its first proprietor, an absolute giant named Louis 'Goldie' Hawkins, whom I invited back in 1996 after I bought the place. So, even though Goldie was the first tenant, his entering my life won't happen until 1996. I can't wait to tell you about that later on.

Now, back to life after Leo and with Wally.

Wallace Pickard, aka 'Wally' had been Leo's manager. Somehow he wound up with the place and immediately renamed it to, what else... Wally's Place. Everyone just called it Wally's. Leo's Place was now Wally's Place.

This next stop along the way would be where I learned my craft for the next 6-7 years. Watching and learning, seeing the good and the bad.

Sometimes, that's just as important.

Wally had been a decorated WWII fighter pilot and was in Pearl Harbor. He was long since retired from the military and in his 70s by then. I have tried to reflect on what I want you to understand about Wally through this story. I like to think about what he taught me.

I had real admiration for Wally. Still do. May he rest in peace.

He was honestly a war hero. The man had literally given up his actual hand for our country. He had (and has) an amazing family for whom I have complete love and respect. You could not find a lovelier bunch of people anywhere. Four generations after Wally and they still spend a great deal of time with us. Wally's great grandson even works for me. We love hosting them. They only get first class treatment at their dad's former joint.

However, if I am going to be honest, like I promised, there was no culture of hospitality. It wasn't his fault. He seemed to fall into it. It doesn't mean he wasn't a great guy. It just means that (from my perspective) he was ill-equipped to be in hospitality, simply because it was a generational thing. Back then, most of Fire Island had a 'captive audience' mentality. He was certainly not alone. Just like the wooden bowls of salad that came with every meal, they were a vestige of an earlier time. I wanted to turn that page.

Today, there are just too many great choices and the hospitality game has properly changed. Reflecting on today, so many of our present Fire Island restaurants now have outstanding leadership and Chefs at the helm. From Mike at Le Dock, Drew at Maguires, Noel at The Sandcastle, Joe at Rachel's and Zack at Hideaway. They are constantly upping their games as the dining culture has evolved. I have reason to think that the early work of Chef Carmen and the amazing succession of talent he helped curate in Chefs Krissy, Wendy, JJ, Joe and Kevin along the way, greatly impacted the food scene on Fire Island. I could not be more proud of them and their passion. They literally lifted the bar.

I hope we are leading the way. Always innovating to give our guests the best memories. Hospitality means creating those memories no matter what it takes.

That's almost exactly why, at age 29, I would decide to buy the building and let his lease expire. I just knew I could create the right culture on a whole new level. I thought that if I elevated the game and brought real world class hospitality to the site, I just couldn't lose. It was worth the gamble. It was, in part, working for Wally that actually made me decide I could take what he created to the next level. I owe him that and more. So thanks Wally. You must be proud of your family.

If Leo was 'the Jewish Danny Devito', then Wally was, 'the mostly cranky, 75 year old Harrison Ford'. He did have a fantastic ace, his girlfriend Edith Mendelsohn. She kept him on a wonderful path, best she could, with her class, grace and wining but quiet personality.

So, at the time Leo passed away and I went to work for his successor Wally, I had been working on Fire Island from about 17-21 years old and it was now my fifth season returning.

In pretty short order, within about a year or two, I was promoted to Bar Manager. Over the next six seasons I would learn my craft, really get to know our guests and even start making mental notes on what could be improved.

I got to work with some of the best in the business there, including: John Sullivan, Brian Beardsley and Jamo Ragusa.

Now it's time to share some fun, one of a kind, bar stories at the heart of why you are hopefully still reading this.

Enter Mr. John Stallupi

Very early on, staff understood that among the many storied, popular and affluent guests who partied with their friends at Wally's, one stood out among all. This was Mr. John Stallupi.

Among many things, John was and is the creator of what people today think of as 'the fastest luxury mega yachts in the world'. John set that trend in motion, except that all his vessels were and are named after James Bond characters, movies and villains. Giant ships with names like Octopussy, For Your Eyes Only, No Time To Die, Miss Money Penny, and 007 were frequently docked right behind the bar. Their arrival was always pure exhilaration and theatre.

His most recent vessels, measuring over 200 feet long, are called Skyfall and Quantum of Solace. Both are worth a Google Search. They can't even fit in the Great South Bay. John remains a visionary in the world of fast, luxurious, high-performance homes on the sea. Check him out #skyfall #johnstallupi.

Along with his immense wealth, reputation, and world-class generosity came occasional interactions with law enforcement. He was a target, at times, for things seemingly rooted in old-world stories of past associates and youthful ventures he had shed long ago. He is the number one car dealer in the USA and is now a builder of mega yachts like no other. One night, I watched him sell 30 million dollars of his classic car collection on TV, only to restart a new collection the same night.

Nonetheless, I got to see one of these intense interactions up close. I will never forget it.

It was a Friday night in June of 1984. I was in my usual spot behind the bar, and we were expecting 'John', the boat, his guests and crew. They didn't just show up. You always knew they were on their way. First of all, the ship started to block the horizon long before it reached the shore. There was always an air of excitement, not just because you knew John was going to literally hand every employee a $100 bill. Just the sheer size and shape of the ship and what could be on the ship always gave it an edge. There was always the chance of an epic night. This particular one would easily fit that bill.

There could be 30 guests or just 4 on the vessel; you just never knew. Sometimes, we would shut the place down and keep it open just for his crowd. They were always polite, easy-going and in a good mood, until they weren't (more on that later).

So, John and his crew, plus about a dozen guests, exited the ship after it docked. As usual, they entered the building with a bit of fanfare, big hugs, and gregarious laughter, plus a lot of $100 dollar bills. The party was starting, music requests were made, tables were getting moved, and the lights were getting dimmed. This was gonna be a great night. I could feel it.

Then, out of nowhere, as if we were in a war zone, helicopters were whirling overhead, and searchlights glared down. The Coast Guard boats had lights and sirens out back, along with FBI men in hats and helmets and some big machine guns all swarming around the ship. Peering out the rear window, I stopped counting at 20 dudes from 5 agencies. You know, the kind with bold letters on their windbreakers.

I looked over at John, and he didn't seem terribly out of sorts or put off by this. He might even be mildly amused at the major tactical operation now surrounding or boarding his vessel.

He calmly walked outside. I could immediately tell that the guy in charge of the operation knew who John was and walked right over to him. They spoke. No one got excited. At least not outwardly. John was so poised. He shook the guy's hand and came back inside, picking up where he left off while two dozen guys with machine guns went through his 'boat' for at least 30 minutes. To the point where they even had two scuba guys in the water under his boat!

About 30 minutes later, the local police came inside and walked out with John to the ship. Apparently, the FBI guy wanted to apologize to John for the 'raid', as they had found nothing but possibly 1-2 registered guns, and they would be leaving. I saw John shake the guy's hand, pat him on the back and walk back inside, where he said, "Let's get this party started!" At that point, all I had to do was put on his favorite song, 'My Way' by Francis Albert Sinatra, and John flashed that full-grin smile to me to say thanks. He loves that song! I miss seeing you, sir. I hope we can break bread someday soon.

The part that stayed with me all these 35 years later is just how calm, cool and gracious he was with all the people who frankly were out to cause him harm. There was a lesson there.

'Skip' - Another John Stallupi Story

This one involves John's good friend, and I think maybe his personal protector, known to us as Skip, who was always by John's side.

It was like a scene out of Goodfellas, except that movie didn't exist yet.

Skip was not a guy to mess with, as you will see. He would be like the Joe Pesci character, except a bit bigger.

However, Skip was not that big. Maybe he was 5ft 10, medium build, and a bit out of shape. Just from good living, I guess. But there was just something about him that screamed, 'Do not fuck with me. Ever."

I was about to find out why he strode so quietly and confidently all the time.

It was the Fourth of July, 1987. Skip stood at the bar, and John and the rest of his guys were outside on the deck, finishing dinner. Skip was facing me, and I was behind the bar, just chatting with him and pouring some drinks, including Skip's Grand Marnier on the rocks, which he was now sipping. The deck outside was starting to fill up after dinner, and the holiday dancing was not far off.

Into the bar walked one of the town's most notoriously angry guys. He was about 6ft 2, had seriously broad shoulders and hands like giant metal garbage can lids. Since it was July 4th, a lot of people were a bit lit, and this guy was no exception. He was a good guy but a nasty drinker. A big, ornery 'Wile E. Coyote' type. No stranger to a bar fight.

He walked up to the bar and immediately to Skip's right. I faced him, so from my point of view, he was to Skip's left. They both faced me. They were shoulder to shoulder. The music was elevated because it was nearing dance time right after dinner.

I grabbed the guy a beer he ordered, and as I handed him the beer, I saw Skip swivel his head to his right and say to the guy, "Nice shirt." It was pretty loud in there, but there's no question: Skip said, "Nice shirt."

Still looking straight ahead at me, the guy said to Skip, "Fuck you."

I glanced over and saw the guy was wearing an American Flag T-shirt, and it was the 4th of July. So, it was clearly a compliment. Plain and simple. No harm intended. Yet.

Quickly, I thought maybe the guy had misheard because it was loud at the bar. He had to have misheard. I hoped.

Also, now I was immediately seriously concerned because I knew who both these guys were, and this was not going to end well. Not a chance. Period.

With that, Skip very, very politely said to the guy much louder now, "Maybe you didn't hear me; I said nice shirt, nice flag!"

The guy swiveled just his neck toward Skip and, looking a bit downward, said, "Fuck you!" Then turned straight ahead, facing me, taking a sip of his beer.

At this point, Skip was still sipping his Gran Marnier on the rocks but now turned his body to the right. Now, Skip said to the guy, "You definitely didn't hear me. I said nice shirt." this time very loudly.

Now, the guy turned his full body to the left, facing Skip, and said, "F…" and before he got the 'K' in fuck out of his mouth, Skip slammed his own forehead into the guy's face.

Split seconds later, and with his catch wounded, bleeding and dazed, Skip had his arms over his head and the guy in an arm headlock. Skip then lowered the guy's head to bar level, his forehead just inches from the bar top.

With little effort, Skip was now pounding the guy's face into the bar rail right in front of me while he was still sipping his Gran Marnier! He pounded once, then twice. Each time, the entire bar shook.

After the first 2 times, Skip took a more slow and measured pace, continuing to use the bar rail as a blunt weapon, maybe 3 or 4 more times. Each time, he paused a bit to take a sip of his drink, looking at me. I'm not kidding. He looked right at me before each slam. As if to say, "This wasn't something I was looking for, but I might as well have some fun."

When he was done, he casually tossed the much bigger, 220-pound fellow to the side, where he slumped over. Skip continued enjoying his cocktail. The police came in and took the bloodied guy outside. Nothing more was said.

It reminded me now of the scene in Bronx Tale where Sonny (played by Chazz Palmenteri) locks the door behind the bikers and says, "Now yous can't leave." You never forget something like that. Rest in peace, Skip!

A Seminal Moment

When I first got started working at Leo's and then Wally's, we had only a jukebox. For those younger readers, this was a giant record player. The guests selected and controlled song choices by paying 25 cents for each song they chose.

The only saving grace with this ancient set up was that I had a 'kill switch' behind the bar to avoid any really badly timed selections. This was pretty frequent. Good song, wrong moment.

Within a short time after my arrival, our GM Greg Grosser and I went to Wally and said, "Look, you want to make some real money here and draw a crowd, especially after dinner. We gotta get rid of the jukebox! Let's put a decent sound system in and clear out some space in the dining room."

Wally agreed. Low risk and high reward at that time. He smartly stepped aside and let some magic happen. One of the best things he ever did while I worked for him.

This was a whole new turning point. We installed a reel-to-reel machine behind the bar (don't make me explain what that is).

I took it upon myself to take a water taxi down to The Ice Palace in Cherry Grove and pick up music from their DJs to bring back to Ocean Beach. I would pre-arrange this every other week or so. I got to know the people at the Ice Palace and made connections that would later bear their own fruit. No pun intended.

This combination of new music, better sound, and more room for guests had an immediate and stunning effect. We were becoming much more than a place to have a meal. The older crowd loved the dance music and stayed after dinner, and a whole new revenue center was born. Almost everyone was happy. Dancing after dinner was instantly popular.

A Brief Side Trip Across the Street

At this point in 1988, I had worked for Wally for 5 or 6 years. Through the efforts of several others and myself, the place was more popular than ever. Yet I wasn't happy. By any standard, though I respected him, it was becoming less enjoyable a place to work.

I wasn't looking to leave but didn't really want to stay.

Then opportunity knocked. Sort of.

The Ocean Beach Grille

So, in 1988, when I was approached by two Ocean Beach homeowner couples to take on a new and expanded role at their newly acquired property, I jumped at the chance. These two couples were and are among my all-time favorite Fire Islanders, and they further set me on a path and direction for which I am forever grateful. The husbands, Marty and Alan, have passed on, but their indelible mark on my memory and career won't be forgotten.

Marty Stamler and Alan Kahn were two New York City real estate developers, and Marty was a brilliant lawyer. Marty was married to Gail, and Alan was married to Judy. They were politically active, super bright and hip. Just the type of people with vibrant, dynamic lives and lovely families that I aspired to have myself. Marty Stamler and Alan Kahn are two mentors I am indebted to, along with others I've mentioned already and some more to come.

I cannot tell you enough how wonderful they were and how good they were to me. I still love seeing Gail or Judy when riding my bike past their houses or in town. Gail frequently comes in for meals, and I have loved watching her daughter and her granddaughter grow up.

So, when the Stamlers and Kahns bought a run-down building diagonally across from Wally's that was a hotel with a bar and asked me to run the bar/restaurant for them, I jumped at the chance. The new place would be called 'The Ocean Beach Grille (formerly Sis Noris, then Dashers and then Le Bistro, and now The Landing).

As part of the process, they allowed me access and real input into their designs, plans, menu ideas, and advertising concepts. To me, this was the first attempt to create a more polished and upscale New York City-type dining experience in OB. Not snobby at all, but clearly more sophisticated. It was my first immersive hospitality experience, from concept to conception. From the ground up. I learned so much. They trusted me with their investment, and they all thanked me when it was over. The surviving wives are still my friends. I think that says a lot about my performance. I hope so.

In 1988, The Ocean Beach Grille was born, and as its GM, I was at the helm. I helped put together the team, which ultimately also led to working with Chef Carmen, who became our original Exec. Chef at Island Mermaid just 3 short years later, in 1991. Chef Carmen was the former Sous Chef at the world-famous Louie's Backyard in Key West. He tutored under renowned Exec. Chef Norman Van Aiken. Carmen was the person who, in my opinion, put Ocean Beach on the culinary map, as far as I am concerned. He remains one of my oldest and closest friends to this day.

That's not to say that OB didn't have terrific food! Places like Maguires, Matthew's and The Bayview or Albatross had excellent food. They just weren't trying to create a dining scene or culture at that time, similar to what I had felt was happening in

NYC. All of Ocean Beach was still handing out old wooden bowls of salad for free with every meal.

Skipping forward for just a second, Chef Carmen went on to run the Island Mermaid kitchen team for over twenty years, creating the lineage, branches and teaching tentacles leading to Chefs Krissy, Wendy, JJ, Joe and Kevin. The lineage is direct, it's real and it's beyond awesome. We love you, Carmen. The OG.

You Look Familiar. Have We Met?

Back to The Grille.

One fine Saturday morning in July, I was sweeping the small, elevated deck in front of 'The Grille'. It was about 10 am. All of a sudden, my greatest hero in hospitality came sauntering up the steps, and he was not alone.

Fire Island is so lucky to have this cat as a lifelong resident down in Fair Harbor. A self-made guy from the Bronx who teamed up with a young Chef named Jean-Georges Vongerichten, or 'Jean-George' to anyone who knows.

Together, they have opened up well over 30 of the world's finest eateries all over the entire globe. If that wasn't enough, this whole thing started as a side hustle! His real business was advertising and making TV commercials, including the famous Michael Jackson one for Pepsi. He has also produced Broadway hits like Kinky Boots.

Phil Suarez is his name. If you don't know him or know about him, you should. A documentary about his life is out there on YouTube. Well worth a watch. Find it.

Here is what The Wall Street Journal once had to say about him.

"You can live in New York for decades and still remain an outsider, blocked from the main action and the big rooms. You know there's a party – now and then, you hear the music – but you can't find it. In this, New York is like the great cities of yore, London, say, or Venice, where hordes of moneymen passed through long enough to make a fortune and a name but remained forever at a remove from the core. In fact, only a handful ever truly possess the place, an elite who were formed by the city and transformed it in turn. They do not announce themselves, but if you happen to meet one of them, you'll know it right away." Wow.

Phil is that guy. Mister NY. Watch the video.

Anyway, so Phil strode onto the deck with his friend and said, "Hey Scott, this is my friend Steve, and we would like to join you for dinner tonight. Maybe about 8 pm. Can you take us?"

Silently, I thought to myself, *Take you? I would move heaven and earth to have you eat here. I might unseat my family for you.*"

I replied, "Of course, Phil. Are you kidding; I'm so glad you could join us. I assume Lucy will be joining you. Will you be four?"

"Yes, four, please." He turned to his guest and said, "Steve's lady is here at the house as well."

Ahhhh. Back to Steve and one of the dumbest things I had ever said to a famous person. It was the only time I'd ever said this, and it will not happen ever again.

Now, in my defense, they were both in sweatpants, and Steve had a baseball cap on.

I turned to the long dark shaggy-haired, barrel-chested, chiseled-nose beast of a man next to Phil and said, "You look familiar. Have we met?" (Immediately sensing it was a stupid question!).

"No, I don't think we have. It's my first time in town, but I'm looking forward to tonight."

They both turned away and took a step when Phil suddenly but very gently turned back, leaned in, and whispered in my ear, "Just don't play any Journey songs tonight! See ya later," patting me on my left shoulder.

Bang, like a ton of bricks, it hit me. A warm little bolt of 'you-are-an-idiot-Scott' anguish ran through my head. Steve Perry, the legendary lead singer of one of the greatest rock and roll bands in America at that moment, was coming to dinner. Not a good way to start my day, but it kinda was.

I never did play any Journey that night while they dined. Especially after my earlier fuck up. However, the minute they left, I queued up 'Oh Sherry' and 'Don't Stop Believing'. It won't be the last celebrity Mr. Phil Suarez dines with at my joint. Years later, he brought the legendary Jean-George himself to Island Mermaid as well. I hope Phil and Lucy join us at Island Mermaid soon. To me, they are among Fire Island's greatest celebrities. Real New York ones.

Before I move on to the next story from The Grille, I would like to say this. I recently, just last summer, got to sit with Phil and his amazing wife, Lucy, for about 15 minutes at his former restaurant Le Dock and took the time to tell Phil just how much he's meant to me as a role model for my own life. Not surprisingly, he had no idea. He seemed quite genuinely moved by my deep admiration. It felt great to get that off my chest.

I was really glad to have found the time to let him know. We should all have the kind of life this guy has had. I wish him continued strength and a vibrant life in the years ahead with his Lucy. Google Phil Suarez Tony Guida's interview on YouTube for more on this NY legend.

Daddy's Toys

Within just one year after helping create The Grille for my friends, they found a big giant fish to buy for (hopefully) ridiculous money. Shit happens. It was a bit hit.

It was now 1989. Enter Aaron Fuchs, a giant man whose only credentials for being in the restaurant business were (1) that he could eat 14 dinner courses plus 5 deserts and still not be full, and (2) he had just come into a boatload of 'fuck you' money from his dad's estate's sale of an entire city block in Manhattan. I had heard the figure was well over a hundred million, split between Aaron and his two siblings. My assumption was that Alan Kahn and or Marty Stamler had met him on the deal. They took the rare opportunity and exited stage left. I was very sad to see them go. I had a bad feeling about 'Daddy's Toy', Aaron. He turned out to be a piece of shit. But it worked out for me.

I agreed to stay on to manage the property and restaurant for him as the new owner, but only if I had a formal contract. Unlike the former owners, I didn't know this guy, and this was a lot of work. He didn't belong in the business and had no connection to the Village. He was a big fat fish out of the water, an outsider. I just knew Ocean Beachers wouldn't like him. So, he really needed me. I needed to be protected. Good thing I was.

I should have known what was going to happen the day I approved the contract, and upon seeing the name of his corporation, 'Daddy's Toy, Inc'. What a giant red flag. I missed it.

The restaurant and bar industry is notorious for its abundance of characters who get involved for all the wrong reasons. This guy was just one more. Plenty of money to park on a vanity play project. I hate those types. They ruin it for all the hardworking industry people in it for a good reason.

Unfortunately, when this happens, it affects a lot of people in meaningful ways. I utterly detest those in this category. Restaurants are not trophies. You don't just open a restaurant because you know how to throw a great dinner party or because you dine out 5 nights a week. It's one thing to make a legitimate investment. It's another to treat it like your toy. Everyone thinks they can and wants to own a restaurant. They think it's cool or sexy until the hard work and shrapnel start. It's not that sexy. Don't do it.

Aaron Fuchs was over 400 lbs and loved to smoke a fat cigar after his third consecutive dessert. As the GM and with a contract that had several key financial milestones, or 'waterfalls' as they are called, I set a rule that a three-course meal was the limit, and if I needed his table, even less. We had some epic challenges and battles with that one. A self-centered, clueless barbarian had invaded Ocean Beach with his 'fuck you' money, and I had to deal with it. What great lessons I learned from this moron.

Nevertheless, at the end of the season, I miraculously hit every single milestone, and he owed me a lot of money. He was not happy.

When it came time to pay up, he tore up the contract in my face and said, "Sue me." He thought that because he had 40 million bucks, I would take table scraps. No fucking way.

I sued him and won. Getting my money and counsel fees. More importantly, I was about to exact some extra sweet revenge. He never got a non-compete clause, and I was about to become his nemesis right across the street. You'll see. Part of my mission was to put him out of business, and I did. Shithead.

Sometimes, the universe has a way of dealing with things.

Karma, Chutzpah and Luck

During that next 1988 season, I heard that the building where Wally's was, was for sale. Knowing that this 'Daddy's Toy' issue was not healthy, I had nothing to lose. In 1989, I went back to work for Wally but with an idea. I found out who owned the building and put together a plan. I now had all the skills to make that plan happen.

In the summer of 1989, while still working for Wally, I went down the street and knocked on the door of George and Lucille Stretch. They lived in the apartment adjacent to where Lucille taught kids swimming for decades in their built-in pool. It's directly across the street from what is now The Pantry. The empty lot.

Hundreds of Fire Island kids learned to swim in that pool. However, lest you get any ideas about Lucille being a soft, warm, mushy momma type, forget it.

They were selling the building where I had worked for Leo and now Wally. Originally, the building was Mr. Stretch's fish market many years prior. They owned many buildings and houses and were part of one of the oldest family lineages in town, maybe on all of Fire Island. 'Original settlers' is how I would describe them.

I had never met them before but had seen Lucille in town several times. She reminded me of 'Aunt B' from Mayberry, except without any of the pleasantries and a German or Swiss accent. I had met George's brother Bob, also an Ocean Beach 'settler', who was the sweetest, warmest gentleman.

Who the Hell Are You?

I went to their house.

Me: *Knock, knock, knock.*

Mr. Stretch: "Be right there, hold on," almost simultaneously opening the door.

Now, opening the door, looking puzzled, he said, "Who the hell are you?"

Nervously, trying to be polite, I explained, "My name is Scott, and I want to talk about your building. Do you have the time?"

Still eyeing me suspiciously, he said, "Come in, take a seat."

I did just that.

Having prepared some ice breakers, I said, "Mr. Stretch, my name is Scott, and I work at Wally's. And for Leo before that. So I am familiar with your building by working there for 7 years. We've never really met, but I'm interested in buying your building. I've done some research, and I'm prepared to make you an offer."

He replied, "You look like a kid and realize I want a million dollars. Where the hell are you gonna get that kind of money?"

"I'm not. But hear me out."

He nodded his head, puzzled perhaps but indicting he will listen, or maybe he was just amused.

"I will give you $50,000." Then I purposely pause. A long pause (now he waited for the good part).

"You will be the bank. I will agree to put $300,000 into your run-down building (I honestly think I used a much harsher word there, like shithole, but it was long ago).

"If I fail after 1-2 years, you'll take back a very improved property. If I succeed, I will refinance and take you out in year 6. We will both know pretty quickly which way it will go." Either way, it's a full-price offer.

And that was my pitch. Let him see the hunger in my eyes. It was quite real.

Having just settled my first big legal case, I only 'had' that much, and the building was in bad shape. It couldn't work any other way, and I had nothing to lose by asking. I expected him to throw me out. If he said yes, I had already lined up the renovation money as well.

He pondered now for a few moments, and before he could answer, I lay two more things on the table, "Oh, and by the way, I'm not paying you 1 million, but I will pay you $995,000 and your mortgage has to be non-recourse." (Meaning, he can only take the building back and not come after me personally).

Now, he is more puzzled. "What's with the $5,000?"

"I don't want to pay extra taxes if it's 1 million. There's a Millionaire's Tax." He saw that I'd done my homework, I thought. I hoped.

He's ready to come back at me now.

"I would agree with your terms, but I've got some of my own. I will hold the short-term mortgage but only 4 years not 5 or 6, and at 14% interest." In those days, 9-10% was pretty normal. The interest rate was 3-4 points more than I considered or wanted to assume. But I didn't hesitate.

Instantly, I held out my hand and said, "You got a deal." He reached out and shook my hand. By the next week, we called in the lawyers. Now, I would have to really earn my place in paradise. This was gonna hurt like hell.

What Am I Going to Call This Place?

Among the myriad and endless details in building the dream, somewhere in that heap of notes and all the scraps of wish lists on paper was an interesting detail. What would I ever call my own restaurant IF I even ever got the chance? And then, there it was. A remnant from an old day dream. Tossed into a brown cardboard box. An old piece of a yellow legal pad with two columns. Column A was all the words that would go with any of the words in Column B. Column A had a list of 20 words like Blue, Happy, Fat, Beach, Island, Fancy and Copper. Column B had 20 words like Marlin, Parrot, Mermaid, Whale, and well, you get the idea. Within 5 minutes, after finding the old list in a cobweb-crusted box, it struck me hard and fast, 'island and mermaid'. One from A and one from B. And so the 'baby' had a name. It even sounded like what I hoped to create! A lovely and mysterious creature all of my own making.

It seemed to fit.

The Island Mermaid Is Born; A Marriage Dies

I gave a lot of thought to the sad parts of this story, thinking, why even put this in here. What's the point?

I have come to realize that I am one of the luckiest guys around, and I got through it. So why not. Of course, in fairness, you check with your family first. Their blessing was all I needed.

Anyway, this is my story, and I get to tell it best I can. There is a lesson here. It's called, 'be careful what you ask for', and that's why it's worth telling. Plus, some more lemons eventually got turned into lemonade.

To 'lay the foundation' as we lawyers say, I have to digress a bit.

During my law school years, 1982-1985, I was still working at Wally's. I continued to work there until 1990, except for that two years at The Ocean Beach Grille, which we will get to.

It was during this time that I would forge a relationship (which turned into a short marriage) with an old high school crush who previously wanted nothing to do with me. Her name was Sue. Not Susan, but Sue.

When we were in East Islip High School, I would see her around. She didn't even know I existed. Trust me, I wasn't alone in that dynamic. Every guy in our school wanted to meet her or date her.

Every high school has 'that girl' (or guy). You know, the one that was 'unobtainable' but you thought in your silly teenage mind, that doesn't include me. The funny thing about her was that she was not at all like the 'cheerleader' girls I had dated. She was in her own category, I think. Her looks might make you think she was fast and loose, but she wasn't at all. Just the opposite.

However, if she even looked your way, your heart might sink, and you would have to remind yourself, "Dude, she's completely out of your league!"

I'm gonna throw out a movie reference here just to end the point. American Pie, starring Shannon Elizabeth as Nadia. Guys, IYKYK.

Anyway, back to the Fire Island story.

So one night, I'm bartending at Wally's. It's now 8-9 years after high school, and in walked, guess who!?

Honestly, I hadn't even really thought about her in the years after high school. As soon as she walked in and up to the bar, it was like I was back in the high school hallways at my locker, looking to my right to catch a glimpse of her at her locker.

Boom, it was game on. But she was not alone. She was actually with a guy we knew from the thriving Bayshore bar scene. A bar called The Golden Leaf. Again, IYKYK. Though I hadn't seen her in at least 7 years, it didn't matter.

Immediately, I could tell from the banter the three of us started that they weren't hitched. They didn't even seem to be a couple. When you are interested, you find a way. My 'game' had gotten much better since high school, I guess.

Like peacocks spreading their plumes, and as any guy might do, I purposely peppered my end of the convo with some tales from law school and my ongoing life and a new loft apartment in the Big Apple.

She peppered her end with tales from post-high school life in Hawaii, swimsuit modeling, and her job as a flight attendant, never once alluding to the now third wheel next to her as her boyfriend. Clearly, they were just friends.

Something was happening here. It was different than my one-sided 'puppy love' high school thing from years past. She was actually paying attention to me. Suddenly, I am thinking to myself, this could actually happen. Maybe. Let's see. Slow down, Scott.

Trying to thread the needle between being interested enough, not being an idiot stalker, taking care of the many other bar guests, and not pissing off 'her date', I had to act fast and smart.

If I got my shot, any opening, I wasn't going to miss it. Don't ask, don't get.

Suddenly, I heard her dinner date say, "I'm hitting the bathroom." (And by the way, this guy was as nice a dude as you might ever meet). Everyone knew he had the same crush on her as I did growing up. We all did.

As soon as he was near the bathroom and out of earshot, I quickly stepped to my left and said, "Sue, look, this is the wrong place and the wrong time to do this, but there's more I need to know about your life. If you give me your number, I want to continue the conversation at a better time for both of us. If you don't leave it, I will know you're not interested, okay?"

I then simultaneously slipped her a pen and paper and walked away. Quickly, I pretended not to really care and kept 'fake busy' just ten feet away.

I waited more than a few seconds and stole a glance at the pen and paper she was now writing on while that warm feeling went from my toes to my head. She folded the paper and slid it to her left and gently in my direction. I strolled past her and took possession of the illicit gift just as Mr. Nice Guy returned to the bar.

Sharing this little secret made the rest of the evening unusually sweet. Even after goodbyes came and went.

At least for the moment, life was good. The completely unobtainable was within reach. Someone should have warned me. I think some tried. I wouldn't have listened. Life has bumps, and this was going to be one of them. A tough bump I had to experience. To make more lemonade.

The Early Years

After graduating law school in 1985 and starting a 2-year courtship, from 1986 to 1988, a doomed marriage was about to happen.

But first, I bought a loft on 18th and Park Avenue South in New York City. This area is known as Union Square. I reverse-commuted to my law office in Long Island 7 months a year and then commuted from Fire Island to my office the other 5 months a year, all while returning in season each night to bartend at Wally's. Those summers and about 35 years more of them continued to be intense 100-plus hour work weeks with these two professions.

It was during those off-season months in New York City and living in Union Square that I really first became aware of the power of hospitality and 'elevated food'. I lived just a few blocks from both Union Square Cafe (Danny Meyer's joint) and Metropolis Grill (Steve Hanson's joint). It was those dining experiences in those two spots that generated my first subconscious and then very conscious thoughts about trying to replicate a small, beachier, casual, fine dining version of what I was experiencing but out in Ocean Beach. To my mind, Fire Island had nothing like it, except maybe The Monster in Cherry Grove. Casual fine dining wasn't really a 'thing' back then. It was either 'fine' or 'casual' as far as I could tell, especially in Fire Island. Over time, I became convinced that there was a real need for a casual, fine dining experience at the beach.

So, as you will see when the planets aligned by meeting Chef Carmen in my 1988 GM role at The Grille and the availability of a prime real estate location on the market in 1990, I knew I had to take the chance. It just felt so passionately right. My head boiled over with excitement. If I could, I was going to help change the culture of hospitality and possibly dining in Fire Island. That was my thought, or at least my dream.

Little did I know how difficult the first three years would be. The nasty combination of the brutally high sellers purchase money mortgage debt service and the slow pace of tilting of the ship in the right

73

direction took its toll. At the end of the first season, I found myself with outstanding debts to six or eight vendors and a potential winter stomach ache that wasn't going away.

I decided on a plan to pro actively reach out to each vendor. I called them. They didn't chase me. I called the meat guy, the fish guy, the bread lady. I told them up front that I only had 50% of their final balance and that if they were loyal to me and let me roll over the modest balances to each, I would guarantee using them for a great many years.

Each of them was gracious and respected that I called them first. It worked. They all agreed to roll me over. Over the next three or four seasons, I caught them all up, and to this day, I still use them as my vendors. By the time of the fourth or fifth season, I could finally begin to see some possible light shining into my dream. It was time to refinance and get rid of Mr. and Mrs. Stretch.

Those were some sad, sleepless winters in the early days. Of course, I was lucky to have kept my 'day job' practicing law to pay the bills. That was only made possible by having an older brother law partner, who allowed me the room to do both. As well as many brutal 100-hour work weeks.

During those early years, my only focus was on how we would continue to raise the bar and find inventive ways to keep our guests talking and wanting more. It was my unspoken rule to be the first to try all kinds of new things provided they also made sense for our guests, our staff, and the goal of attracting a wider audience. I always called these new things 'game changers'. We had to have more than one each year. We still do. I insist on it.

Game changers took and still take all kinds of forms. It could be almost anything, big or small, that gave our guests a better experience, made us a more interesting venue, broadened our appeal, or just something that made working less stressful for me or our staff.

Gerry Lynas: The 1st Game Changer

Once the name Island Mermaid was selected, I wanted to do something a bit dramatic that would both capture some attention and begin to create a culture. Something that had never been done at the beach. I remember seeing a giant Buddha at the entrance of a Tao dinner in New York. In one of those moments that are hard to describe, I had a dreamy epiphany of sorts. I decided I wanted a giant, life-sized mermaid above the bar as our guardian or mascot, like the Buddha but beachy.

I remembered a local visiting artist on the beach in Fire Island named Gerry, who occasionally created magnificent 2 story-high sand sculptures. He would spend 10 hours on these sandy works of art and then let them wash away.

Crowds would gather to see his intricate, hauntingly intense work. He would conjure up sea serpents, Greek gods, and gigantic castles and make them come alive for the kids on the packed beach. Just watching him work was a treat. Please take a look at his massive talent at Sandsong Art. Or Google Gerry Lynas. The man is amazing. Pretty sure he was an early inventor of the frisbee! The internet is chock full of his massive works.

I did some research and asked around. I found Gerry's contact and explained who I was and what I wanted. I appealed to the artist inside the man. At this point in his fabulous career, large companies would pay him handsomely, and I had no money to pay him. Not yet. But, what I did have was his love of Fire Island and his desire to help someone struggling to use his art.

Somehow because of his adoration for all things Fire Island, Mr. G. Augustine 'Jerry' Lynas, a famous sand sculptor, agreed!

However, like any true artist, he had two conditions: (1) that my then wife, Sue Funk, pose for the original small clay sculpture he would use to create our mascot mermaid and (2) that he be allowed to finish the work in Fire Island with sand from our beach. It had to be Fire Island sand !

The deal was struck.

He would build her in the basement of his Spanish Harlem apartment building. When he was done, we would arrive in NY City by a pickup truck, pick her up, tie her down in a flatbed, and take her along the ocean to the beach to The Mermaid.

The plan also had Gerry arriving just days later to finish her up while on a scaffold, using only Fire Island sand.

It was during the move that something a bit magical happened.

On a beautiful April evening in 1991, four to six of us arrived in Spanish Harlem in two trucks and pulled up to Gerry's building. He had already had his neighbors help bring the giant creation up to street level. We also knew we had to time the trip to coincide with the beach tides for the ride back to Ocean Beach.

As we pulled up to his building, there was a crowd of children on the sidewalks and in the street. Gerry, who was also a documentary filmmaker, had his camera out. Some of the children were crying. As we approached, I found Gerry and asked him what was going on and why there were all these kids, not to mention why are they crying?

I looked around and saw quite a few tiny tears and small kids pointing at the sculpture. They were 'crying in Spanish', so it was unclear to me what was happening.

So Gerry explained to me that these kids had watched him bringing the Mermaid 'to life' in the building, and he had to tell them she was leaving to go to her new home. They didn't want the mermaid or 'sirenuse' to leave. They were sad but wanted to say goodbye. It was a touching moment and an omen. The mermaid itself, like the Buddha, could touch people. She could stir them.

I think now about how these kids are probably 40 years old with their own kids! I wonder what they remember from that night. I will never forget it, or Gerry.

Always Looking For Game Changers

In our first years, we created Bayfront Aerobics before lunch with the wonderful Anne 'Funky Fitness' Niland and my GM, sister Nancy. We had Acapella Nights with the legendary Freddie Frogs and Karaoke (before it was a thing) with John and Suki. Whatever it took to make the venue interesting and not just about great food and warm hospitality.

One early food-related game changer also has a funny story to it.

In our second year, we got the idea to combine food presentation with raw building materials as a playful way to make food even more interesting. So, I said to Chef Carmen, "I want to do several items but serve them in a way that combines the use of actual earth-like building materials."

We decided on 3 materials to start: copper, marble and cedar.

It was agreed that he would create a Portabella Polenta Stack that would be housed inside a big copper tube, and the tube would be removed table side to reveal the warm moist mushroom stack.

It was also decided that our desserts would be served on oddly shaped polished marble blocks of all colors. So I would go to the quarry and explain my crazy idea to the Italian craftsmen. They loved it. So they let me personally throw heavily chipped marble slabs into a pile and take whatever odd shaped pieces broke off. Man, were they heavy.

Lastly, it was decided that our steak would be finished and served on a cedar plank shingle. Thankfully, each of these was a big hit.

At that time, in the summer of 1992, not much of this was the norm, at least not to my understanding. It didn't matter. Chef Carmen loved it, as did our guests. In my mind, we had created something interesting. We had elevated the game. Keeping to my dream.

One night that winter, I was watching Johnny Carson. In those days, a frequent guest was celebrity Chef Emeril Lagasse. This was Emeril in his prime. In his segment, the Chef introduced the audience to his new Cedar Plank Trout as a way to serve it to his guests at Emeril's down in New Orleans. Emeril was using the cedar plank to showcase the fish. Fantastic! Maybe we were on to something. Maybe, before Emeril.

I called Chef Carmen immediately and jokingly told him to turn on his TV. That Chef Emeril had 'stolen his idea'. I remember us both being really elated at the time, and we shared a laugh. It made us realize we were in a good place and getting better. We were elevating the game. That's all that mattered to me. Keep it interesting. Make it joyous for our guests.

Here is what the Times-Picayune said about Emeril's new restaurant that winter of 1992. "One holdover from Emeril's Spunto is a wood-burning oven...a 'jambalaya pizza', and PLANK ROASTED trout."

Chef Carmen, who remains one of my dearest friends, still laughs about this with me when we get together. As Emeril would say, "Bammm!"

More Than a Bump in the Road

Life briefly came to a halt during the final months of my first year owning and operating Island Mermaid.

I had great reservations about putting this on paper. Yet, it was another seminal moment that ultimately led to more lemonade, including having the blessed family I would go on to meet, make and have. It's hard to segue without mentioning the end of a marriage and what happened.

I figure I will type it out, and then if I don't like it or it's too painful, I will edit or delete.

You will recall that I said, "No one warned me about being too excited about capturing the full attention of my swimsuit modeling high school crush."

In context, it is true that during my first year of operations, I literally worked round the clock. It could, I guess, be fairly argued that I neglected my other role as a new husband, but only in the sense that work was all-consuming. Two jobs, either of which could crush someone.

There were many nights when I woke up in the dining room, with the birds chirping outside at 6am, my face planted in a pile of paperwork. Though a truly worthy cause, not a great recipe for a healthy marriage. Guilty as charged, but not sorry.

What I did not see coming, and what I was blindsided by, was what came next.

Tensions were clearly mounting, with the more than occasional outburst of 'you care more about the restaurant than me' behaviors. Perhaps deserved. Clearly misplaced.

So, one day in August, after I hadn't seen Sue in a couple long work days, I decided that I needed a grand romantic gesture to fix up this growing impasse. I knew she was on the mainland at her sister's house, but she wasn't answering my calls.

I had decided that I would rush off the island, grab two dozen red roses, have lunch and spend the day with her. Showing her that I could actually take a break from the hardest job I had ever encountered. A job, by the way, she had equally signed up for. Two jobs.

I called her sister and confirmed she was staying there, though her sister was at work. I raced off the island, stopped at the florist, grabbed 24 roses and drove east to Sayville. I was gonna go get my girl. Make things right.

I pulled up to the house. I knocked on the door. No answer. Yet, I could hear something.

Carrying the roses, I walked around to the side of the house. I could suddenly hear voices. Plural.

Now my heart was racing. I listened more closely, and I heard one female voice and one male voice. I hear a shower running. This isn't good.

I threw down the roses and lifted and slid open the bedroom window. Now, the voices were clearer. One male, one female. Through the fog of rising distress and anger, I now knew the intended target of my growing rage and uncontrollable insanity.

I climbed through the window and fell into the bedroom, the voices from the bathroom still uninterrupted. I rushed over to the bathroom door and listened for just a second or two. It was a conversation between two people, one of whom was my wife, and the other was strangely familiar. The level of rage was peaking now. My heart was pumping outside my body. I heard it in my ears.

I turned the door handle and popped open the steamy door.

There, outside the shower, wrapped in a white towel under her armpits and facing the mirror, was my bride. She turned to her left, now facing me and became as white as the towel. Eyes wide open.

I moved forward very fast while the now one-sided conversation was still coming from the shower. I pulled the shower curtain sharply to the left, and there was my 6ft 3-inch waiter.

Our eyes connected, and instantly, he was cowering in the corner, water shooting everywhere. Rage filled my eyes and my soul.

Quickly, I ran into the kitchen to find the biggest knife in the house. On the counter was a wooden block of cooking knives. The kind with many choices. I grabbed the big one and darted back into the bathroom. My target was still cowering in the corner. I rushed up to him and raised the knife way above my head.

Just as I was about to lower the blade somewhere, she grabbed my wrist from behind and begged me to stop, shouting, "It's not what you think, it's not what you think."

For reasons no one could understand, I stopped. I had to listen to this. Thank god I did. I am now no murderer.

For the first and only time in my life, I understood how someone charged with murder might just have a real defense. Like you read in the papers.

Anyway, even then, my stupid brain didn't understand it was over. I wanted to believe otherwise. It's not uncommon.

Remarkably, and I guess to her credit, she went on to marry that guy and have 3 absolutely beautiful boys with him. At least one of them is a pretty famous fashion model. She actually fell in love while I wasn't looking.

It was the best thing that ever happened to me. It was time to turn the page. I would find my own true love about 7 years later. Standing right in front of The Mermaid. My Jaimee girl. More lemonade!

Small Town Politics

The politics of Ocean Beach have, over time, been central to my orbit. I can't deny that, and frankly, I am extremely proud of whatever role I have played. However, I think it's important to understand the why and how.

This could be boring, but I feel very passionate about the subject. It's a small town, and many feel just as passionate as I do. And they should! I'm glad they do.

The best decisions come from the middle, not the right or left. The OB political pendulum had swung too far in one direction. I would help be part of a group that would bring it closer to the center.

Young people, pay attention here.

The actual road that houses the political lanes of traffic led me to some of my favorite mentors, including what I call 'The Four Mayors': Arthur Silsdorf, Tom Schwartz, Jim Mallott and Natalie Rodgers. Each of whom, in their own special ways, left an enduring, positive and specific set of marks on my mind and heart. I call them The Four Mayors, but they are each remarkably different. I will speak to them below.

But first, I want you to know how it started. It's the only way to understand the entire picture. The passion. Those reading this might take some things for granted. Please don't. Here is that story. I hope it helps you understand why and how I got involved. Past may be prologue.

One morning, while at the Mermaid, circa 1993 or 1994, I was looking out the front window on the street side.

There, near the corner sitting on a bench was a man and his son. The boy seemed to be about 10 years old. The man was eating something and drinking from a coffee cup.

A police officer arrived and confronted the man. I assumed it was about the then existing no eating and drinking rule. Ahhh, The Land of NO. What this man was doing was, in fact, illegal. Period.

You see, at that time, it was illegal to eat or drink on Main Street or, as we call it, Baywalk. I know it's hard to believe. You got ticketed or arrested for eating a bagel. You couldn't bike ride or BBQ either. Let's take that in.

You got ticketed or arrested for eating outside or riding a bike. BBQing was out of the question.

The exchange between the two men seemed bumpy but not physical. I could not hear the words, but very quickly, the guy was being cuffed in front of his son. Perhaps, he was complaining about not knowing the draconian rules. He certainly never became physical.

My heart sank. The young boy was in tears.

For those of you reading this and thinking, "No way this happened." I can tell you. It did.

I thought to myself, how can I own a business here with that type of interaction. Right outside my door. I was just stunned. Sure, the man was technically breaking the law. No doubt. But there just had to be a better way. The image left me shaken and stunned.

But that wasn't the end.

Then, a month later, in the same season, I got my new tax bill. When I opened it up, I almost fell on the floor.

In the commercial district, we have an excess sewer and excess water line item as well as an excess Third Day garbage pickup fee on our tax bill. The average taxpayer probably doesn't know that.

We can argue about the merits of those items, but what comes next is unarguably hostile. This wasn't about money. This was about revenge.

The town board and its then Mayor had gone ahead and summarily tripled our water rate and quadrupled our sewer rate, only in the commercial district.

My excess water bill line item went from about $3000 to $9000, and my sewer charge line item went from $4000 to about $12,000. Wow. $7000 excess fees went to $21,000. Not the tax bill. Just the excess fees.

I decided at that moment I should look into this and get involved. It seemed punitive at a minimum. I knew it was the 'Land of No', but this was now the land of No Way to me.

I decided to become politically active. God forbid a guy with a local business and a lawyer as well should ever do that. Honestly, I felt castigated at times but pressed on.

Over the next few years, I found that a group of like-minded beautiful souls was working for some common sense political change. That group, and my involvement within it, led to some amazing changes, which everyone now just honestly takes for granted. To be clear, I'm not taking credit here.

I'm simply saying that without the effort of many, including Sally and Mike Potterton, Alan and Judy Kahn, Gail Stamler, Jim Mallott, Natalie Rogers, Andy Miller, Robin and Louie Citronetti, Suzie and Donny Cafuoco, and a half dozen others, you might still get arrested for eating an ice cream cone, riding a bike or turning on your BBQ! That's a fact. Screw anyone who says otherwise. I was incredibly proud to be in the company of these citizens and neighbors. These local warriors.

Remember, though, the changes were hard fought, with a lot of friendships being lost and vitriol spewed. You would not begin to imagine it until someone got up at the town board meeting holding a baseball bat and said, "If one of you hits my kid with your bike, this won't be pretty!" Or, you hear them say, "The smell of a BBQ is horrible; we can't have it."

Things like bike riding and the ability to BBQ at your house are just two small examples. A pension program for our volunteer fireman and the ability to eat a bagel on Main St., previously controversial, to say the least, came into being.

We could legitimately argue about a lot of political things, but not those. They are common sense changes that we all now routinely enjoy. We still need some rules and better social behavior for sure, but let's please never return to the Land of No.

Getting rid of the 'Land of No' moniker given us by The NY Times was, in my mind, a very worthwhile thing. Most don't know the tortured history grounded in trying to legislate reasonable behavior in a tiny community that had gone too far.

I want you to know and remember that.

I also want to keep the charm of small-town life. They are not incompatible. Don't let the pendulum swing too far in EITHER direction. Stay in the middle.

Those early stories would take their own book. Stories about having my signs measured weekly with a measuring tape and getting off the ferry in my lawyer's suit and tie, being confronted with each day's big stack of tickets, still make me nauseous remembering it. The absolute audacity of guys like former Mayor Mike Youchah and his cronies is unforgivable to me. We in the downtown were purely a revenue stream for him and his cronies. I worked my butt off to get him defeated when he ran for re election.

I stayed in the game and served for 6 years on 'the board', becoming the youngest ever elected trustee at that time. It was really hard juggling two professions, two very young boys, home life, and the role I had wanted in the village. I have Jaimee to thank for agreeing to allow me to do it.

I would like to take a few moments to at least acknowledge and thank the people who have had the biggest impact on my life in this political area, though. Please allow me that opportunity.

The Four Mayors

Only because we are in the 'politics' section of this book. Each of these OB Mayors happened to be hugely influential in my life. The best of the best.

Arthur Silsdorf. A giant of a man though small in stature! A brilliant lawyer and someone who worked hard and made a lot of money at the beach. He showed me a path to combine both a law career and a business. Like him, as a lawyer, I have represented a lot of local commercial enterprises and homeowners for over 35 years. At one point, he probably represented 80% of all the business owners and or landlords. His trademark hat and bow tie, along with his chompy cigar, will never be forgotten by me. He was a wise-cracking Groucho Marx, Damon Runyon's character.

As a young lawyer, commuting daily to my office or court and racing back here to operate my business, we had time for many discussions about the balance of beach life and the law. We hit it off. I found him to be full of great advice and catchy one-liners (one of which I asked his permission to steal and still use every single day). Really, every single day.

He and I would often talk about the law and agree that there are just some things (like good taste) that you can't legislate. I miss him. I wish he was still here to call me 'kid'.

Thomas 'Tom' Schwartz. If ever there was someone whom I admired for his brilliance and ability to get things done, it was/is this guy. We didn't always agree politically, but most of the time, he was right. We share a deep common love of the law, this island and the need to preserve its character. His towering intellect, combined with his unwavering love of our island, led to some good conversations and opened my eyes to bigger-picture concepts and ideas, including a great respect for the difficult quality-of-life issues on our tiny island paradise.

His impact on my choices is clear to me. Despite the very vibrant nature of my business, I am always mindful of my neighbors and the community because of him. Not a bad legacy. I so enjoy it when he and his family walk from Loneliville to dine at The Mermaid.

James Mallott. Our current multi-term Mayor. Jim Mallott has been a father figure to me. He always has the most brilliant yet simple and straight-up advice. The delivery is flawless and to the point. Blunt, when necessary, but always kind and forthright. I have the deepest admiration for his commitment to our Village and the things he has accomplished on our behalf. Not many could have handled both Sandy and The Pandemic the way he has. Kudos, Mayor Jim. God bless your wonderful family. Though, when you need something out of the box, go to Betty!

Thanks for always allowing me to voice both agreement and disagreement or anything in between. Your own Fire Island story is remarkable, and more people should know it. You were supposed to leave 50-plus years ago at the end of your first season too!

Natalie Rodgers. Perhaps no other woman, except Arlene Jaffe, has had a role model influence on me than her. Feisty, fearless, ferocious, yet kind and generous of spirit. She taught me the art of compromise without giving away your principles. Her famous line to me, which I very often repeat to others is, "When you win, shut up."

Her personal legacy to me includes the idea that when you want something done, ask a woman. Rest in peace, my friend. I won't soon forget you. I heard you passed today at 103 while I am writing this, so a tear was shed on this page. I think you are looking down on me. Much love, Natalie.

Back to Fun at the Mermaid

Over the years, some pretty cool celebrity interactions have jumped into my lap. I would love to share a few that stand out, such as moments with Mark Messier, Keith Hernandez, Barbara Corcoran, and Boomer Esiason. There are quite a few celebrities living on our island, and we all tend to just give them their space. This isn't the Hamptons, for Christ's sake. That's how it should be.

On the other hand, it can make for some ultra-interesting moments. Here are just a few.

Keith Hernandez

For the uninitiated, Keith was one of the most famous Mets baseball players and a real NY guy. After his exciting career, he continued to be a sports broadcaster. His fans were rabid, including, at the time of this little story, my then Executive Chef, Joe Rago.

I'm pretty sure that Joe still has a poster of Keith in his Mets uniform above his bed. Or, by now, his son's bed. It's gotta still be there.

So, one day, my friend Bobby Devine of NYC China Club fame told me he was coming for an early dinner with Keith. They were close friends. It was probably about 1997 or 1998.

After they arrived and settled in, I approached Keith.

"Keith, I need a small favor."

"Sure, Scott. What's up?" Bobby looked my way nervously from across the table.

Breaking the ice, I told him, "Keith, my chef might be the biggest fan of yours on the planet, and I think he still has your poster over his bed."

He laughed...still waiting for the ask. Thankfully, the whole table laughed.

"I want you to follow behind me into the kitchen, and when his back is turned, pop out from behind me and say, 'Chef, where the fuck is my steak!'"

Thankfully, Keith loved the idea. As did his table guests. So, he followed behind me, and we walked into the kitchen.

In the middle of the ballet dance that was a Saturday night, Keith popped out and did his thing! Everything stopped. Eight or nine bodies pivoted his way, including Chef Joe.

Chef turned around and literally jumped up on Keith, almost dry-humping him. He probably delayed that hug 5 seconds too long. What a blast. The smiles and high-fives lasted a long time. I was glad I could do this for Joe. Keith made his summer.

Barbara Corcoran

Who doesn't know and adore Barbara these days? She happens to be a Fire Islander, to boot. Her role on Shark Tank is a master class. This one happened in about 2014, I think.

Regulars know every year for 33 years, I publish a newsletter we give to every guest. Like I said, the idea came from copying Danny Meyer at Union Square Cafe. This one year, I put Barbara Corcoran in the newsletter. Just a two-line blurb. "Did you know Barbara Corcoran is a Fire Islander?"

One day, Barbara showed up for lunch. The newsletter went down on her table like anyone else. I saw her glancing at it. She's a 5 ft 1-inch tiger. All of a sudden, she called out across the deck, "Scott, I want to see you. Come over here now." Like I was Mr. Wonderful!

Nervously, I walked over, hoping all was fine. I already knew why she was calling me. She looked up at me from her seat and, with a straight face, said, "Nice newsletter, but I want a royalty for every one," tapping the newsletter for extra emphasis. For about 2 seconds, I almost peed my pants. Then she laughed. So I laughed. I think. When she left, I thanked her for being a good sport about it.

Keeping in character, she said, "I'll be back for my money!"

Mark Messier

Again, I can't assume everyone knows this legend. One of the greatest ice hockey players to ever lace up a skate. Moreover, he's one of those true NY role models, like 'Derek Jeter'. He helped take The NY Rangers to the top of the heap. The Stanley Cup.

So, in about 1998, one day, Mark was here for lunch with some friends, and this was back when he was near his famous peak. I was sitting with him, talking about lacrosse, of all things, and he was telling me how he really loved the game because it had similarities to hockey.

As we talked, all of a sudden, I turned around, and there was a line of kids and their fathers and mothers in a queue with sharpies in hand. I excused myself and got up to go look, and I saw the line was almost around the block.

I came back to Mark and let him know. I asked him what he thought we should do. He said, "I'm gonna sit here and sign every single autograph no matter how long it takes." And he did. I don't know who was happier, the kids, the moms, or the dads. What a gentleman.

Boomer Esiason

Most regulars know that I met Boomer in high school. Again, if you don't know Boomer, you should. He is the hardest-working post-All-Star career athlete around. Forget that he was a NY Jet/NFL/Super Bowl quarterback.

He is one of the busiest football commentators we have and a radio talk show host on The Fan with Boomer and 'Gio', Greg Gianotti.

Beyond that, he founded a charity to find a cure for Cystic Fibrosis and raises tens of millions of dollars a year all over the country. Doing it all as a loving dad and role model. His efforts have helped extend the lives of thousands of people, including his own son, Gunnar.

For quite a few years, we threw a small, fun 'gala' charity night for his foundation, and on those nights, things became electric for a few hours. When Boomer decided to not only bartend but also throw footballs to the dance floor for $100 donations, the crowd loved it.

However, this was only topped when he was asked to throw one into the Great South Bay on a hook pattern being run by an event guest diving into the water. One ball $500.

Boomer hit him like a bullet in the chest from 50 yards. I thought the guy was gonna drown! Go Redmen! We miss those special nights. Thanks to both Boomer and Gio for the support you couldn't ever pay for.

The Twin Disasters

We all gathered near the TV in NYC, watching as the eye of the murderous superstorm took a terrible last-minute left turn, knowing then that Fire Island was ground zero for Sandy. We would not be spared. Just the opposite. This was going to be an apocalyptically horrific direct hit. And it was.

All we could do was pray. We wanted to know that those who stayed on the island were okay. We had friends who would be there to save the beach.

It would be about 2 weeks before we could come back. In the interim, social media showed horrible videos and images of our Village, including a rushing river of water from the ocean rolling past The Mermaid and into the Bay. That's when I knew it was biblically bad. I assumed it was probably over.

As is often the case with Fire Islanders in tough times, we rallied. On the island, the men and women of OBFD, OBPD and EMS, Village staff, and The Mayor, Mayor Jim, got to work. Fast. Some of you may have forgotten. Please don't.

A daily convoy of supplies needed to go over, and a group of us would shop, take supply requests and pack boxes to send over to those incredible first responders and contractors. Whatever they needed, we got. Cigarettes, gloves, Jameson, bags, shovels, socks, beef jerky and hats. We were not alone. It felt good to help.

Round trips from Manhattan to Costco to the Ferry were done several times each week. I did them, as did many others. It was the least we could do. We felt helpless, so this gave us some purpose and welcome feeling of community.

Once we got back, there was no time to waste. No time to feel pity or sadness. Just work. Just keep digging away the blackness one inch at a time. No time to process the magnitude.

I remember sitting on a milk crate, feet covered in mud, weeping my way out of a nervous breakdown. Feeling alone. In the dark. With only my wife on the other end of the phone to console me and get me moving.

Disaster Two, a COVID Story or Two

As we entered the early stages of Covid restrictions, we had to react fast. In the earliest stages, I had to quarterback hard. Be decisive.

We turned the dining room into a delivery triage space and made it super easy for guests to order online or navigate in person. We used 'gorilla tactics' to market ourselves and relied on the goodwill of our loyal guests, built up over 30 years. We took the most extreme steps we could to protect our staff and guests. The Wall St. Journal did a piece on what we were doing to handle the difficult divergent aspects of safely running a restaurant during Covid.

Things got very sad for our team and me early on when we lost two prior team members from summers past to the disease. These were friends of ours.

I want to give a warm shout-out to the families of both Jason Weinger and Andre Guzman. Both were part of our longevity and success. Jason was one of my first managers many years back. He was younger than me. It hit me hard.

This sent me into a tailspin that I almost didn't get out of until my whole family told me they were leaving the beach if I didn't get help. Bleaching the entire house was no longer going to be tolerated. Eventually, I came around and used the power of my poetry writing to get through it.

I thought hard about whether one single Covid story could sum up how hard the entire process was so not to dominate this book.

I thought about what we came to call 'Cuomo Chips' and turning our dining room into a takeout triage. I thought about removing and measuring tables 6ft apart and plexiglass safety transformations overnight.

But here is the one story that tells you all you need to know about the difficulties we dealt with daily while trying to stay open. The one story that, in one form or another, happened dozens of times.

The State had made a rule that you could sit with a drink in your hand as long as you ordered food, but dancing was forbidden. You had to stay seated. On its face, it seemed beyond odd to us. Yet, at its core, I understood its larger purpose. Whether I agreed or not didn't matter.

The Covid virus didn't know if you were sitting or standing, eating or not eating, but we rationalized it and obeyed the rule, to the point of physically removing some who decided they wouldn't listen. We took it literally and seriously. It caused serious tension night after night.

One night at about 11 pm, a couple walks in, followed by about 8-9 young girls who seemed to be about 16 years old. Immediately, I approached the couple to find out how I could help since the kitchen was closed. It was rather odd during peak Covid that any large group would walk in, let alone underage persons, and at that time of night.

When I asked the couple how I could help, they informed me that it was their daughter's sweet 16, and the girls were so couped up at home they just wanted to listen to some music on the bay. They asked if the girls could please stay if they stayed with them. Just to be outside and listen to music.

I felt bad for them and said yes, under two conditions. First, no drinking, and the parents had to stay. Second, as crazy as it sounds, no dancing. We decided to play fun, upbeat music during Covid, and almost everyone loved it but followed the rules. It was a social compact between us and our guests.

They said they knew about the rule and would happily comply. Everyone won. Or so I briefly assumed.

The moment I turned my back, all the girls started dancing, and the father started laughing.

I turned back to the father and said, "Maybe there is a misunderstanding; we agreed no dancing, right?"

He said yes, looked at the girls, and they stopped. Until I turned away, and they all started dancing again.

I know this seems funny now, but at the time, you could anger a lot of the wrong people doing this, including some OB homeowners who were calling the NYS Liquor Authority. Everyone was on edge.

Now, I turned back and saw one of my security guys heading toward the father. I motioned to hold up. I got this. Security stayed nearby. He watched me and the father.

I said to the father, "Why would you put me in a position like that when I'm helping you make the best of your daughter's difficult Sweet 16 weekend? Now, you all have to leave. Now."

With that, he turned to me, pointing his angry finger, and said, "You fucking Democrats are ruining this country; you're all sheep!!" (As if I somehow had a giant D painted on my forehead). I let security walk him out.

That's what running the business during Covid was like. Non-stop tension and misplaced anger.

The Best Night Ever - COVID and All

Unlike the first Covid story, this one represents the best thing that happened to me and The Island Mermaid guests. It leads to one of the single greatest nights of my Fire Island life. Lemonade.

So, one day, I got a call from a longtime friend Ira. Ira Zahler. Known locally, just as Ira. Or DJ Ira. IYKYK.

Ira told me that his friends, whom I also knew, had their band gig canceled at the last moment. If I recall, the cancellation of the indoor event was Covid related.

Would I consider having them play on the outside deck? And by the way, they were traveling and playing with the new lead singer for INXS.

Whoa. What? Did he just say that the new lead singer for one of my favorite 80s bands wanted to play at my bar?

For those younger readers, INXS had monster songs, you know. Songs like Devil Inside, Never Tear You Apart, Suicide Blonde and Beautiful Girl.

Let me tell you something. The band, even without the new lead singer for INXS, was already killer. We had them once before, and it was lit.

When I heard that they added what might be a once-in-a-lifetime singer to the mix, it was the biggest no-brainer in a long time. People were dying for some safe outdoor entertainment. Fire Islanders would never see a group of this caliber in Fire Island. Only indoor Covid cancellations created this. Time to squeeze some lemons.

Then Ira said, "You don't even have to pay them. Just buy them dinner."

It took 3 seconds to make that happen. Done.

What happened next was magical.

When I say magical, I mean it.

You ever see a band tuning their instruments and already know how insanely powerful and tight they are? Even as the band was just warming up, you could see our guests in rapt attention. The sound check blew them away. Guests started texting their friends, 'Get down to The Mermaid'.

It might as well have been Rodger Daultry up there.

The lights went down. Within ten seconds of the opening song, it was game on. No one took their eyes off them. Voices like that, who have played stadiums like Wembley, The O2, or Madison Square Garden, don't just play on the Mermaid deck. Ever. Only Covid caused this, and the generosity of Ira and the band. They just wanted to play. Somewhere. Outside.

The stars glowed that night, both in the sky and on stage. Jaws were dropping, and cameras were poppin'.

I was in music heaven. But, somehow, it got much, much better.

After several encores and the late hour, they said goodnight. Everyone went home. But the show, the real show, wasn't over.

Sitting around just to cool off and decompress both from pure Covid fatigue and the miracle of what just happened, one of the guys says, "Do you mind if we break out the acoustics and play for ourselves?"

It was midnight. Just the 6 band members, Ira and me. We formed a socially distanced circle of chairs. Guitars in hand, rocks glasses full, it begins. They even handed me a tambourine.

One of the guys says, "Any suggestions?"

The cockney-laced response was, "Mate, let's do the Beatles' White Album start to finish first." The White Album, in sequence, a brilliant idea.

I'm sitting next to the raw talent equivalent of Aerosmith's Steven Tyler, and the voice is the best I've ever heard at that close range. Not the best voice ever. Just by far, the best voice I've ever sat next to.

Once the Beatles catalog was run about, someone said, "How about some David Bowie?" After that, how about some Neil Young, Van Morrison, Springsteen and Stones.

Blues, Motown and Marvin Gaye.

This went on for almost 4 hours. Adam, another friend, sat in and joined us.

We had all been so Covid fatigued we didn't give a fuck what time it was. We didn't want the music to stop. We were outdoors, socially distanced and free. We left planet Earth, and its troubles for 4 glorious hours.

For that brief night, we had a rest from Covid. I had my life back, at least until the next day.

Louis 'Goldie' Hawkins

Let's go back in time now.

Here is what The NY Times once said about my next piano-playing character:

"Mr. Hawkins, noted pianist and restauranteur in Ocean Beach and New York City, died Thursday, March 16, 2000, in West Palm Beach, FL. Goldie retired to Palm Beach 25 years ago, where he continued to entertain for 20 more years at various private functions. He was known and loved by thousands."

Years prior to buying The Mermaid Building, by complete coincidence, my then father-in-law and I had bought a house on Bayberry Walk. Two from the ocean.

Though we didn't buy it from Goldie, it was sold to us by the person who did buy it from Goldie. It was Goldie's original home, and it was called Magnolia Alley. By virtue of who lived there, it had achieved its own status and notoriety. Goldie lived there with some very famous friends.

It was in this first context that I learned a bit about him before later buying the location of his famous restaurant.

In a tiny town like ours, everyone has a story about the history of your house. Neighbors and even the broker and seller recalled how Goldie lived in the house with his famous celebrity friends, including Broadway star Ethel Merman, Honeymooners TV star Art Carney and Movie star Dudley Moore. That's how I came to learn that Goldie owned 'Goldie's' on the site where Mermaid stands today.

Shortly after buying the home, my former father-in-law and I did a renovation. Part of the renovation called for tearing out a drop ceiling in the living room, which we would also call an attic space or crawl space.

One night, while tearing out the ceiling, all of a sudden, a huge pile of treasure trove hit us in the head. Treasure trove is what actual lawyers speak for, "Finders keepers, losers weepers." Among the vast and incredible things secretly left behind in the attic by his housemate Ethel Merman was an Al Hirshfeld lithograph of Annie Get Your Gun signed by the entire cast, including Irving Berlin; personalized invitations to the White House from Presidents Nixon and Eisenhower; dozens of personal stage photos with her celebrity peers of the day, including Bert Lahr, Jimmy Durante, Bob Hope, Sid Caesar, and Henry Fonda; hundreds of records and master recordings; and my favorite, a warm love letter from John Steinbeck on his personal stationery. Pure treasure trove.

Also among the treasures were Goldie artifacts from his OB namesake restaurant. So the Goldie glow was known to me in that setting long before buying 'his location' downtown. His Goldie's restaurant menus, with the trademark watermelon logo, were among the fabulous finds.

Fast forward years later, when I coincidentally purchased the building which housed his former restaurant, I knew about the legend pretty well.

When I first bought The Mermaid Building, I continued to hear a non-stop rumbling about this guy 'Goldie'.

Older guests would chat about Goldie this or Goldie that. It got to the point where I had to find out more. Who the hell was this guy? All I knew was that he was the original owner of the place I just bought, before it was Leo's Place and Wally's.

Then, I got a crazy idea. Why not ask Goldie to do a reunion at The Mermaid!? If so many loved him, we could recreate a Goldie's Reunion night. A win-win-win for everyone.

Who else to turn to but Arlene Jaffe (again) for advice on finding Goldie.

I called her.

"Arlene, I need to know more about this guy Goldie. All anyone talks about is Goldie and The Goldie Days. People tell me that he was a real one-of-a-kind raconteur who lived in Ocean Beach. He was likely the first openly gay business owner in town. Is he still alive?"

At the mere mention of Goldie, Arlene's voice broke. Broken but with a kind of nostalgic joy. The good broken.

Arlene: "You want to talk to Goldie, let me know. He lives in Palm Beach, and I have his number. I keep in touch with him even though he left Fire Island in 1975. Let me give you his number."

It's 1996. I have my idea on paper. Two shows. One at 6 pm and one at 8 pm. Goldie's Reunion Watermelon Logo Shirts with a 3-course meal, assigned seating, and advance ticket sales. $100 pp and Goldie at the piano entertaining his former guests again. I'm ready to pitch the idea. I call him up.

Given who he was, I was super nervous.

"Goldie, my name is Scott, and Arlene Jaffe gave me your number. I bought the building where your beloved Goldie's was in Ocean Beach, and I've operated it for 5 years. All I ever hear is Goldie, Goldie, Goldie. I would love to have you back here for a reunion. Arlene has your old piano and has agreed to lend it for the night. Would you possibly consider it?"

Goldie: "Darling, that sounds rather interesting, though it might cost you a bit of money. Let me ask my friend Arlene about you. We can speak again soon."

Not long after that, a deal was struck, and he agreed to fly up for a one-night performance. $2500. Ads were taken out, tickets were flying out the door, and within weeks it was an absolute, unequivocal sellout. Every single 10-top table was taken, and every single seat had a guest name attached to it in

106

my 'war room'. 120 seats, times two shows, 6 pm and 8 pm. 240 happy Fire Islanders.

Chef Carmen, also a proud gay man, understood the assignment and, as was his manner, crushed the concept, even putting the original Goldie watermelon logo into each course on the menu.

Watermelon. Why watermelon? Because, as Goldie told me, "Darlin, I'm the biggest fruit on the island!"

Darling, I'm Not Coming

Weeks after the show was sold out, I got a call. It was the man himself. Foul-mouthed, southern accent and all. The reunion show was about ten days away. The T-shirts were piled up in my office.

Goldie: "Son, it's Goldie. I'm not comin'."

Me: "Goldie, sir, may I ask why?!"

Goldie: "Because son, I didn't like those sons of bitches, and they sure as hell don't like me. I'm not comin'."

(It is probably true that he had his detractors because he was blunt and feisty! But he had no idea how many Ocean Beachers adored him)

Thinking quickly on my feet now, knowing I've got a completely sold-out event, I shifted gears.

Me: "Goldie, can I tell you a quick, true story that just might change your mind?"

"Sure son, go ahead."

"Goldie, beyond the event being completely sold out, I got a call from a woman named Mrs. Ostrowsky the other day. She's in her 70s now. But when she was in her 20s, she would sneak down to your New York City nightclub just to sit next to you at the piano when her husband went off to the Merchant Marines. Between us Goldie, I think she was secretly in love with you. She's coming from California to Ocean Beach to see you. You can't disappoint people like her!

Then, with his trademark bluntness and southern twang, he said, "Darlin, I didn't like pussy back then, and I certainly don't like it now."

However, to my delight, he then said, "But I like you son, so I'll be there. Just have my envelope good 'n' ready because I don't know you from a hole in the wall." I handed him his envelope when he got off the boat and walked up to the restaurant.

And so after leaving Ocean Beach in 1975, he showed up 20 years later in 1996 to see all the regulars from Goldie's and play for them in two back-to-back sold-out shows during two separate 4-course meals.

Chef Carmen made 30 piano-shaped cakes (one for each table for both shows) to celebrate. Like I said, each course had an element of watermelon built in. All in honor of the one, the only, the legendary Louis 'Goldie' Hawkins.

At one point during the middle of the first 'set', I noticed there was no piano playing. Nothing.

I turned my head towards Goldie, sitting at his original piano, which Arlene had lent us, and I had re-tuned. He's talking to a line of guests at the piano and

108

signing old photographs of them when they were little kids.

Silly me, thought I hired a piano player. So, I start to walk toward the legend. I didn't even get within 10ft of the piano, and he spun all the way around and stopped me in my tracks with one look. He looked through me and said, "Son, I'll be playin' when I'm good 'n' ready." I turned tail and walked far away. He was the man.

The funny thing is that he wasn't so much a piano player as he was an iconic figure. The first openly gay businessman in Ocean Beach and apparently a take-no-prisoners badass. He was 'the celebrity to the celebrities of his time'. In Goldie's (now Island Mermaid), on any given night, his housemate Ethel, 'There's No Business Like Show Business' Merman, or Marilyn Monroe could be at the piano signing with him. Some of you might recall a show called The Honeymooners with Jackie Gleason also. The 'Norton' character was Art Carney, Goldie's OB housemate as well. Ocean Beach was a mecca for artists, musicians and actors in those days. The legendary Bert Bacharach played his piano at the Bayview, where the Albatross is now. You would see Carl Reiner and Anne Bancroft in town or at Goldie's.

It was such an honor to host him. By the end of the night, he said to me, "Son, you put together a wonderful evening. Would you do me the honor of having breakfast with me and Jim tomorrow, please?" This thrilled me to no end because it was a complete affirmation of the intense work surrounding the Goldie Reunion.

When we met for breakfast and started eating, he said, "Son, we're gonna play a little game I like to call dead or alive. I'm gonna call out a name; these are my old patrons, and you just tell me if they are dead or alive!"

Me: "Yes sir, no problem."

And he proceeded to call out about two dozen names. Each time, I would let him know their fate. Dead or Alive.

For many of my responses, he pounded the table, saying, "I knew I'd outlive that son of a bitch!" I thought it was pretty funny. Goldie, the man adored by tens of thousands of his guests, had his own 'short kill list'.

Seems about right, I think, and funny.

Rest in peace, Goldie.

Epilogue

As I near the end of this road trip down memory lane, I'm starting to think, have I left anything out? Are there stories I'm missing? What do I want to leave you with?

The answer is yes. It's been a long ride, and I don't want to blather on too long. Plus, forgetting things is just an unwelcome part of the process.

I had to pick an imaginary place to stop, though frankly, I could keep going. I told my sweet wife Jaimee that I was going to give her the best gift ever, and leave her out of the story. She couldn't be happier. And so I will, except for one short story.

Moreover, it's a great place to end. Ending where it all began.

Second Chances

I was at the bar about 7-8 years after creating it. I looked out front and saw my tenant and friend, Steve Wald, chatting with a dreamy little goddess of a woman. She was in a tight turquoise top and had the sweetest smile. It was one of those inexplicable moments where your heart set you in motion before your mind could think. I bolted out front and walked up to the two of them.

"Steve, aren't you going to introduce me to your friend?"

"Yes, of course, this is Jaimee."

We've been together ever since.

She is 100% responsible for making me a potential human being. Though her favorite bars are Housers and The Tross, this book is dedicated to her.

Appendix A – The Covid Poems

COME SEPTEMBER

That time of year
We hold so dear
What will it bring
Instead of Spring
Come September
The month we mend
At Summers end
Stolen days on the beach
Now seem out of reach
Come September
Truth be told
We would welcome the old
When seasons journeys end
Suns rays always last to bend
Come September
Come September
I hope we remember
It was our common bond
Which got us beyond
Come September
And perhaps to December
Our families will arrive
And keep us alive
As the next few months start
They might break us apart
So many voices, so few choices
No one rejoices
But if we come together
Even this cane we can weather
This fragile place
Gives us our space
Come September

Homework Blues

I wake up every morning
Wipe a salty tear from my eye

A warm bead of sweat
Rests patiently upon my brow

Thought I heard my teacher last night
She's was looking for my homework

Oh, teacher tell me what you want
Wants to see it right about now

She's not angry or upset
Her disappointment still makes me fret

Her face is hazy and hard to see
The voice still resonates with me.

Haven't been to school
Least not in close to forty years

Never missed a day of class
Follow the rules and you'll succeed.

Always did what I was told
Step out of line and it's you they'll scold

I need your structure and your fire
What else leads me to inspire

You were always the one I could please
Now, I fear idle hands disease

Teacher, teacher I got the blues
Got no direction from which to choose

Isn't tomorrow another school day
Or have I already lost my way.

Does anyone even still care
What I have to say.

When I wake up in the morning
Don't want to sing the homework blues

When I wake up tomorrow morning
A brand new direction I will choose

Nowhere To Go

It dawned on me
The other day
And today again, haphazardly
I have no where to go

Crossing borders
It's not the time
Puddle jumpers
Wait in line

But, do I need to travel far?
Not if I just take the car
Life is fine, stay at home
Yet my soul aches to roam

Is it just risk - reward ?
No where I can't afford
Factoring in the mental state
Why is it I just can't wait

Am I living in the wrong place?
I shouldn't need to replace this space
Because I do - maybe it's true
Might be time to move

Is it really greener there?
Are the sunsets just so splendid?
For what is my dream intended

Tear no more pages from magazines
Searching the globe for my dreams
While coming apart at the seams.

Perhaps I can "fix" this place.
Just by bringing in a tiny new face

Water, Wind and Waves: A Thanksgiving Ode to our OBFD

Winter waters wash and crash
Along the Bayfront walls they smash
Winds whip-in hard from the North
Winter waves roll in like mountain rocks
Not how we left you in the Fall
Soon, it won't be how we recall
Hide your faces and don't look up
Get there fast, no time to stop
Life's about to "unforgive"
Thanks to you volunteers
We have chosen here to live
You see us in the Summer shine
With our lovely glass of wine
On the beach or by the pool
Warm breezes to sip, staying cool
But this island has another side
From her grip you can not hide
Dewy morn gives way to icy storm
And the wood burns all night long
There's work to do that's for sure
Don't believe the summer lore
They make it hard for good reason
Winter here ain't your season
Takes a raw and hearty bunch
Barrier island packs a puncha
Yet, you are here at the ready
Someone has to hold her steady
When you hear that alarm bell ring
Her horn rings loud that's the thing
Bike or cart, it's to the fight
No matter if it's day or night
Your teams jump forth to get it right
Most of us are out of sight
For generations present and past
You hit the gear and don the mask
Operations both small and large
One of you is always in charge
Someone brings the battle gear
Stepping up with no fear
And so it goes year after year
Until we see you in the Spring
We already know the honor you bring
You keep us safe and feeling proud
Just had to say this all out loud
Much love and warm respect
Scott, Jaimee, Luke, Carson.

The World That's Dim But Grows Not Dark

Look now out upon the shore
Look long and hard
Far beyond your door
In every corner of every place
Help us heal both time and space
Filled with hope and gentle breeze
Not just the bay but upon the seas
Let's be real and embrace the pain
Only then will our hearts refrain
Sing the song of great battles won
So our dearest may sit in the sun
This is not our "locked in" place
No silent army can invade our space
America is still too full of grace
In the marathon of the race
Leave this time with little trace
Lift me up and I will you
Rally like our brothers past
Sisters and soldiers at the mast
Around the bend and over the hill
This dream for our children we must fill
Only if we eat bitter pill
The world is dim
But grows not dark
Lighting the flame of billowy bark
Treasure the small and forgotten place
Take comfort in every little space
Steal the look upon their face
The arc of time will bend toward joy
But now our humanity we must deploy
Bring your enlightened spirit to the task
Surely you know why we ask
It's not hard to wear a mask
Help us grow the future bright
Never a more worthy fight
Dim's not dark so shine your light.
It's more than just being polite.
It's about doing what's right.

The Light Is Always On

We take this short pause -
This brief hiatus

The days cool down
The nights grow longer

We rest our souls
To come back stronger

Summer 2020, was like no other
Shoulder to shoulder, brother to brother.

Never will we take you for granted
In your seats firmly planted.

For 30 years you stayed by our side
Making you happy fills us with pride

Our loyal, magic army of fans
You bring your kids, family and friends

Locals, renters, owners and all
Our only concern is you have a ball !

You come by boat, foot or bike
Our hospitality is what you like

Next we greet you, and we will
We promise you an amazing thrill

God willing and if it's meant to be
Your smiling faces we can't wait to see

Once inside you'll feel our embrace
Maybe then we can see your face !

From the moment we take our break
We start to plan the next steps to take

For 30 years we've had one tradition
No closing up without that condition.

Close up each night but never gone
That single "light" is ALWAYS on.

So rest assured, we got twenty - twenty WON. ♡
It's going to be some crazy fun !

Though we've dropped the last check
We say thanks with warmest respect

Made in the USA
Columbia, SC
24 February 2024

04a93980-bc6d-4cac-87d7-bfeb9e474b85R02